THE

YACHTSMAN'S

HANDBOOK

A CLASSIC HANDBOOK ON SAILBOAT HANDLING,
SAILING PROCEDURES, AND WATER ETIQUETTE.

BY **HERBERT L. STONE**
ORIGINALLY PUBLISHED IN 1912

LEGACY EDITION

THE CLASSIC OUTING HANDBOOKS COLLECTION
BOOK 17

Doublebit Press

*Originally published in 1912 by Herbert L. Stone.
Doublebit Press Legacy Edition ISBNs
Hardcover: 978-1-64389-190-3
Paperback: 978-1-64389-191-0*

*WARNING: Some of the material in this book may be outdated by
modern safety standards. This antique text may contain outdated
and unsafe recreational activities, projects, or mechanical,
electrical, chemical, or medical practices. Any use of this book
for purposes other than historic study may result in unsafe and
hazardous conditions and individuals act at their own risk and are
responsible for their own safety. Doublebit Press, its authors, or
its agents assume no liability for any injury, harm, or damages to
persons or property arising either directly or indirectly from any
content contained in this text or the activities performed by
readers. Remember to be safe with any activity or work you do
and use good judgement by following proper health and safety
protocols. In addition, because this book was from a past time and
is presented in an unabridged form, the contents may be culturally
or racially insensitive. Such content does not represent the
opinions or positions of the publisher and are presented for
historical posterity and accuracy to the original text.*

*DISCLAIMER: Doublebit Press has not tested or analyzed the
methods, materials, and practices appearing in this public domain
text and provides no warranty to the accuracy and reliability of
the content. This text is provided only as a reprinted facsimile
from the unedited public domain original as first published and
authored. This text is published for historical study and personal
literary enrichment purposes only. The publisher assumes no
liability for any injury, harm, or damages to persons or property
arising either directly or indirectly from any information
contained within or activities performed by readers.*

INTRODUCTION
To The Doublebit Press Legacy Edition

The old experts of the woods, mountains, and farm country life taught timeless principles and skills for decades. Through their books, the old experts offered rich descriptions of the outdoor world and encouraged learning through personal experiences in nature. Over the last 125 years, handcrafts, artisanal works, outdoors activities, and our experiences with nature have substantially changed. Many things have gotten simpler as equipment and processes have improved, and life outside, on the farm, or on the trail now brings with it many of the same comforts enjoyed in town. In addition, some activities of the old days are now no longer in vogue, or are even outright considered inappropriate or illegal. However, despite many of the positive changes in handcrafting, traditional skills, and outdoors methods that have occurred over the years, *there are many other skills and much knowledge that are at risk of being lost* that should never be forgotten.

By publishing Legacy Editions of classic texts on handcrafts, artisanal skills, nature lore, survival, and outdoors and camping life, it is our goal at Doublebit Press to do what we can to preserve and share the works from forgotten teachers that form the cornerstone of the authentic and hard-wrought American tradition of self-sustainability and self-reliance. Through remastered reprint editions of timeless classics of traditional crafts, classic methods, and outdoor recreation, perhaps we can regain some of this lost knowledge for future generations.

On the frontier, folks made virtually everything by hand. Old farmers' knowledge and homestead skills were passed on to the future generation because it meant survival. In addition, much of traditional handcrafts and outdoors life knowledge was passed on from American Indians – the original handcrafters and outdoorsmen of the Americas.

Today, much of the handcrafted items of the frontier are made in factories, only briefly seeing a human during the process (if at all). Making things by hand indeed takes much (often strenuous) work, but it provides an extreme sense of pride in the finished job. Instantly, all hand-made items come with a story on their creation. Most importantly, though, making items with traditional methods gives you experience and knowledge of how things work.

This is similar to the case of camping and the modern outdoors experience, with neatly arranged campsites at public campgrounds and camping gear that has been meticulously improved and tested in both the lab and the field. These changes have also caused us to lose this traditional knowledge, having it buried in the latest high-tech iteration of your latest camp gadget.

Many modern conveniences are only a brief trek away, with many parks, campgrounds, and even forests having easy-access roads, convenience stores, and even cell phone signal. In some ways, it is much easier to camp and go outdoors today, and that is a good thing! We should not be miserable when we go outside — lovers of the outdoors know the essential restorative capability that the woods can have on the body, mind, and soul. But to experience it, you need to not be surrounded by modern high-tech robotic coffee pots, tents that build themselves, or watches that tell you how to do everything!

Although things have gotten easier on us in the 21st Century when it comes to handcrafts and the outdoors, it certainly does not mean that we should forget the foundations of technical skills, artisanal production, and outdoors lore. All of the modern tools and cool gizmos that make our lives easier are all founded on principles of traditional methods that the old masters knew well and taught to those who would listen. We just have to look deeply into the design of our modern gadgets and factories to see the original methods and traditional skills at play.

Every woods master and artisan had their own curriculum or thought some things were more important than others. The old masters also taught common things in slightly different ways or did things differently than others. That's what makes each of the experts different and worth reading. There's no universal way of doing something, especially today. Learning to go about something differently helps with mastery or learn a new skill altogether. Basically, you learn intimately how things work, giving you great skill with adapting and being flexible when the need arises.

Again, to use the metaphor from the above paragraphs, traditional skills mastery consists of learning the basic building blocks of how and why the old artisans made things, how they lived outdoors, and why woods and nature lore mattered. Everything is intertwined, and doing it by hand increases your knowledge of this complex network. Each master goes about describing these building blocks differently or shows a different aspect of them.

Therefore, we have decided to publish this Legacy Edition reprint in our collection of traditional handcraft and outdoors life classics. This book is an important contribution to the early American traditional skills and outdoors literature, and has important historical and collector value toward preserving the American tradition of self-sufficiency and artisan production. The knowledge it holds is an invaluable reference for practicing outdoors skills and hand craft methods. Its chapters thoroughly discuss some of the essential building blocks of knowledge that are fundamental but may have been forgotten as equipment gets fancier and technology gets smarter. In short, this book was chosen for Legacy Edition printing because much of the basic skills and knowledge it contains has been forgotten or put to the wayside in trade for more modern conveniences and methods.

Although the editors at Doublebit Press are thrilled to have comfortable experiences in the woods and love our modern equipment for making cool hand-made projects, we are also realizing that the basic skills taught by the old masters are more essential than ever as our culture becomes more and more hooked on digital stuff. We don't want to risk forgetting the important steps, skills, or building blocks involved with each step of traditional methods. Sometimes, *there's no substitute for just doing something on your own, by hand.* Sometimes, to truly learn something is to *just do it by hand.* The Legacy Edition series represents the essential contributions to the American handcraft and outdoors tradition by the great experts.

With technology playing a major role in everyday life, sometimes we need to take a step back in time to find those basic building blocks used for gaining mastery – the things that we have luckily not completely lost and has been recorded in books over the last two centuries. These skills aren't forgotten, they've just been shelved. *It's time to unshelve them once again and reclaim the lost knowledge of self-sufficiency.*

Based on this commitment to preserving our outdoors and handcraft heritage, we have taken great pride in publishing this book as a complete original work without any editorial changes or revisions. We hope it is worthy of both study and collection by handcrafters and outdoors folk in the modern era and to fulfill its status as a Legacy Edition by passing along to the libraries of future generations.

Unlike many other low-resolution photocopy reproductions of classic books that are common on the market, this Legacy Edition does not simply place poor photography of old texts on our pages and use error-prone optical scanning or computer-generated text. We want our work to speak for itself and reflect the quality demanded by our customers who spend their hard-earned money. With this in mind, each Legacy Edition book that has been chosen for publication is carefully remastered from original print books, *with the Doublebit Legacy Edition printed and laid out in the exact way that it was presented at its original publication.* Our Legacy Edition books are inspired by the original covers of first-edition texts, embracing the beauty that is in both the simplicity and sometimes ornate decoration of vintage and antique books. We want provide a beautiful, memorable experience that is as true to the original text as best as possible, but with the aid of modern technology to make as meaningful a reading experience as possible for books that are typically over a century old.

Because of its age and because it is presented in its original form, the book may contain misspellings, inking errors, and other print blemishes that were common for the age. However, these are exactly the things that we feel give the book its character, which we preserved in this Legacy Edition. During digitization, we did our best to ensure that each illustration in the text was clean and sharp with the least amount of loss from being copied and digitized as possible. Full-page plate illustrations are presented as they were found, often including the extra blank page that was often behind a plate and plate pagination. For the covers, we use the original cover design as our template to give the book its original feel. We are sure you'll appreciate the fine touches and attention to detail that your Legacy Edition has to offer.

For traditional handcrafters and outdoors enthusiasts who demand the best from their equipment, this Doublebit Press Legacy Edition reprint was made with you in mind. Both important and minor details have equally both been accounted for by our publishing staff, down to the cover, font, layout, and images. It is the goal of Doublebit Legacy Edition series to preserve America's handcrafting and outdoors heritage, but also be cherished as collectible pieces, worthy of collection in any person's library and that can be passed to future generations.

Every book selected to be in this series offers unique views and instruction on important skills, advice, tips, tidbits, anecdotes, stories, and experiences that will enrichen the repertoire of any person looking to learn the skills it contains. To learn the most basic building blocks leads to mastery of all its aspects.

The Yachtsman's Handbook

THE
YACHTSMAN'S
HANDBOOK

On the Practical Equipping, Care and Handling of Boats

By
HERBERT L. STONE,
Editor of "Yachting,"
AND OTHERS

Illustrated with Diagrams

NEW YORK
OUTING PUBLISHING COMPANY
MCMXII

CONTENTS

The Yachtsman's Handbook

The Yachtsman's Handbook

THE PROPER NAVIGATING EQUIP-MENT.

APPARATUS REQUIRED FOR THE PROPER AND SAFE OPERATION OF SMALL CRAFT, INCLUDING THE U. S. GOVERNMENT REQUIREMENTS.

BY CHARLES H. HALL.

THE proper navigating equipment for yachts and motor boats depends somewhat on the size of the boat and largely on the extent of her cruising ground and the character of the waters in which she may operate. Nevertheless, there is a certain minimum outfit that should be on hand always if any cruising is to be done.

THE COMPASS AND ITS LOCATION.

First and foremost is the compass, and a good one from a reliable dealer will prove best in the end. True, a good compass costs real money; but there is an old adage about "spoiling the ship for a ha'p'orth o' tar" that should be borne in mind. A small, single-needle dry compass is often more of a hindrance than a help, especially in a small, lively boat; while a well-made liquid compass, with a large, clearly marked card, will give a feeling of security in fog that will amply repay one for the money expended. The best makes of dry compasses, with light card and many needles, equal the liquid compasses in steadiness and sensitiveness, but cost as much as the corresponding sizes of the liquid ones.

In making a long run a card as large as 6 or 7 inches in diameter will allow much greater nicety of steering than a small one, as with a 7-inch card one can steer to a degree, while with a 2 or 3-inch card the boat can scarcely be kept within a half point either side of her course. The binnacle, or box containing the compass, should be of hard wood, brass or copper, without any iron or steel in its structure, and should be arranged for proper illumination at night. The majority of binnacles are lighted with oil lamps, though some have been put on the market lately with electric lamps. Care must be taken that the light is thrown on to the card and not in the helmsman's eyes, and is not too bright. A binnacle is now on the market with a tiny incandescent lamp of only 35/100 candle-power. In any case, double shutters sliding across the after part will be found useful. For day running the shutters are thrown back or the binnacle hood removed entirely; for night work the shutters are brought almost together, leaving but a narrow slit through which the lubber's line and an inch or so of the card may be seen. If the binnacle hood is removable the azimuth instrument may be used for taking bearings.

The location of the compass should be given considerable thought in planning a new boat, so

Wooden boat binnacle with electric light

that it may be close to the wheel, in a commanding position, and as far removed as possible from the disturbing influence of iron and steel. In fitting a compass on a boat already built there is little choice left, as it must be under the helmsman's eye as he stands at the

wheel. The center line of the binnacle shown
by the "lubber's line" must be strictly fore and
aft, and should be in the center line of the boat,
if practicable. Keep all steel and iron away
from it, as well as the spark coil and electric
wiring. Do not stow a shot-gun, marlinspike,
frying pan, or other similar object close to the
compass, even if a bulkhead or deck intervenes,
and expect it to be unaffected. A boat davit
that swings in or out within ten feet of the
card will affect its direction. Iron skylight
hinges will affect it, though they may be covered
up with paint, and so unsuspected. A steel shaft
in the steering gear may be a hidden snare.

On a small open launch the binnacle is usually
of the type known as the "boat binnacle," with
fixed top, one sloping side of glass and no
shutters. Such a binnacle is usually stowed in
a locker when not in use, but should have chocks
fitted to receive and hold it securely when
needed for steering. A cabin cruiser generally
has the binnacle permanently secured and of a
more elaborate pattern than the boat type. A
compensating binnacle with removable head
will be the most convenient and useful. The
fee paid to a professional adjuster for compensating its errors will purchase much peace of
mind during the season and prevent worry as
to whether "the deviation should be applied to
the right or left." The whole subject of com-

pass error should be carefully studied, for the needle points *true* north in few spots on the earth and *magnetic* north very seldom when not properly adjusted and compensated.

CHARTS.

Next in importance comes the chart, or marine map, which shows the coast line and channels, sand banks, reefs, ledges, and other dangers; lighthouses, lightships, beacons, buoys, rangemarks, etc., all classed as aids to navigation; and the depth of water and nature of the bottom at all points. The U. S. Government charts are the best and clearest, and should always be used, taking pains to get the latest issues and not trusting to one two or three years old, as channels and shoals often shift, buoys and lights are sometimes changed in location or characteristic, new ones established, lighthouses abandoned, fog signals altered, and so on. A marginal note, "Aids to navigation corrected to (date)," should always be looked for. The U. S. charts are so cheap that there is no excuse for going without them into strange waters.

The stowage of charts in an open boat is always a vexing problem, as the rolled chart is an abomination to use and the flat one takes up valuable space. The writer has seen this prob-

lem solved by cutting the charts into sections
about 10" x 14", glueing a section on each side
of a thin board and covering the whole with a
transparent, waterproof varnish. Boards only
¼ inch thick and made of three sheets of
veneer will be found useful, but should receive
a coat or two of paint, especially on the edges,
before mounting the charts. On a cabin boat
a proper chart table should be provided, with
soft pine top and several shallow drawers at
least large enough to take the chart when
folded once. If space is at a premium, the
blank margins may be cut off and several inches
gained. The chart table should be readily accessible from the helmsman's post. A chart
frame with soft pine back and glass cover will
be found most useful on deck, especially in wet
or windy weather. The chart should be
fastened to the back by thumb-tacks, and the
glass cover should have a rigid frame that will
swing up and be held up by a catch when plotting courses or bearings. The whole may be
permanently secured near the steering wheel or
arranged to drop into chocks, being stowed
below when not wanted.

For plotting bearings on the chart, laying out
courses, etc., a parallel ruler, 15 or 18 inches
long; a good pair of dividers, 5 or 6-inch size,
and a fairly soft pencil of triangular or hexa-
gon section and an eraser will be required. The

dividers and the mountings of the ruler must be of brass, german silver, or similar non-corrosive metal, as steel would soon rust in the dampness of a boat. Have a little shelf for them over the chart table, or a small drawer for them and the azimuth instrument, and keep them in their proper place when not in use. Get good instruments from a reliable dealer and take care of them. Narrow bags filled with sand or fine shot will keep the edges of the charts from curling up when stowed in the drawers. Always keep the charts in the proper order, and, if folded, mark the number and name on one of the corners next the front of the drawer.

AZIMUTH INSTRUMENT.

An azimuth instrument will be found invaluable for taking bearings, whether of the sun or of some terrestrial object, such as a lighthouse. This is an apparatus of bronze that slips on the glass cover of the compass bowl with a projecting lug that fits into a depression in the glass and centers the instrument. At either end a sight vane hinges up, a stop limiting its travel, one vane having an eye-piece, sliding up and down, and the other a vertical wire and a blackened mirror that may be swung up or down. A horizontal wire crosses the center of the base

in line with the vanes, and a small spirit level
is fitted at right angles to the line of sight.
When in use the instrument is set and centered
on the compass bowl, the sight vanes swung up

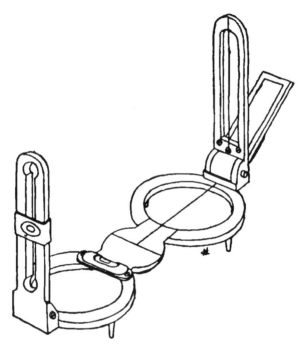

Azimuth instrument for taking bearings

until vertical, and the apparatus revolved until
the vertical wire, when viewed through the eye-
piece, bisects the distant object. Now looking
at the card, the horizontal wire will be seen
against a division, and the direction is easily

read. When not in use the vanes are folded down and the instrument may be left on the bowl, ready for use at a moment's notice, or stowed in its box and kept at hand. It is a necessity when swinging ship for compass error or when accurate bearings are wanted, and is inexpensive. Some of the more expensive metal binnacles have revolving hoods fitted with vertical wires, but to my mind the azimuth instrument is far handier to use.

LIGHTHOUSE BOOKS.

To identify lighthouses, buoys, etc., the lists published by the Lighthouse Bureau should be obtained. One of these, the "List of Lights and Fog Signals on the Atlantic and Gulf Coasts," gives full information about every lighthouse, lightship, lighted buoy and fog signal on those coasts. Another, the "List of Buoys, Beacons and Day Marks," covers all the unlighted aids to navigation. These books may be obtained *free* from your chart dealer or by writing to the Lighthouse Bureau at Washington. The various volumes of the "Coast Pilot," published by the U. S. Coast and Geodetic Survey, gives much valuable data about channels, courses, dangers, tidal currents and kindred topics, and cost but fifty cents each, durably bound in canvas.

THE LEAD.

The lead and line is used for finding the depth
of water at any spot. The hand lead should
weigh from seven to fourteen pounds, and the
line may be ten or twenty fathoms long. The
lines should be well stretched before marking,
and the marking must be done while the line is
wet. The present system of "marks and deeps"
is antiquated, and a more convenient lead line
for the average motor-boat navigator would
have every fathom marked up to five, with the
feet marked up to two fathoms. Getting accurate soundings with a light hand lead requires
considerable practice, especially if the boat is
traveling 10 knots or so. For navigating rivers
or shallow bays a 10-foot sounding pole may be
used, with each foot marked and numbered.
The marks should be carved into the pole and
the numbers also, so that they may be *felt* at
night. Roman numerals—I, II., etc.—are sug-
gested. For the same reason the marks of the
lead line are of different fabrics, such as leather,
calico, serge and flannel. Do not forget to
allow for the stage of the tide when comparing
soundings with the chart.

TAFFRAIL LOGS.

When making an extended cruise with long
daily runs through open waters, the patent log

will be found a most useful device, especially if
fog be prevalent. The usual form consists of
a rotator, which is towed at the end of a long
line and revolves as it passes through the water.
This rotary motion is transferred through the
line to the recording mechanism, which has dials
with pointers showing the distance traveled. It
should be read every hour, and also every time
the course is changed or a bearing or sounding
taken. It should be hauled in before entering
a harbor, to avoid damaging the rotator by con-

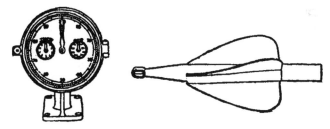

Taffrail log, showing dial and rotator

tact with oyster stakes, buoys, or other objects.
The rotator must be taken aboard carefully and
not allowed to swing against the boat's side, as
a very slight bend in a blade will vitiate the
readings of the log. Another form of log is
now manufactured where dial shows *speed*
instead of *distance,* and is actuated by the pressure of water caused by the boat's forward
motion. If the engine revolutions are known
and data for a "speed-revolution curve" are at

hand, the distance run can be obtained by noting engine revolutions and elapsed time. Many of the Sound steamboat lines navigate thus in thick weather; but, if the draft of water varies much from that when the data were obtained, this method is hardly reliable. A well-made patent log varies very little in successive runs over a course of fixed length and with the same length of line. The maker should be consulted as to the proper length of line to use, as this differs with the size and speed of the boat.

For ocean cruises sextant, chronometer, nautical almanac and tables must be added to the above list; but for the usual coast-wise port-to-port run the equipment specified will be all that is required.

GOVERNMENT REGULATIONS FOR MOTOR BOATS.

The U. S. Government requirements for motor boats are contained in the Pilot Rules and in Circular No. 207, issued by the Department of Commerce and Labor, which contains a copy of the act of Congress approved June 9, 1910, and certain Regulations by the acting secretary of the Department of Commerce and Labor. The current circular is dated February, 1912, and should be studied by everyone interested. The act defines the words "motor boat" as including "every vessel propelled by machinery and not more than 65 feet in length, except tugboats and towboats propelled by steam." Motor boats are divided into three classes by over-all length, class one including all boats less than 26 feet, class two from 26 to 40 feet, and class three from 40 to 65 feet.

The running lights to be carried "in all weathers from sunset to sunrise" are as fol-

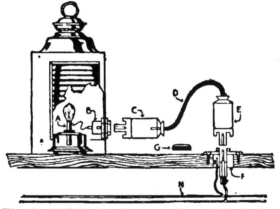

Electric sidelight, showing connection and deck plug

lows: Class one, a white light aft, to show all around the horizon, and a combination lantern forward showing green to starboard and red to port through ten points of the compass each side from right ahead to two points abaft the beam, the white light to be higher than the colored lantern. These lanterns may have plain glass, but those for boats of class two or three must have fresnel or fluted lenses. Classes two and three must carry a twenty-point white light forward "as near the stem as practicable," showing through ten points on each side and with lenses not less than 19 and 31 square inches area, respectively. Also, a ten-point

Standard for holding stern light on small, open boats

light each side, green to starboard, red to port, with lenses not less in area than 16 and 25 square inches, respectively. In addition to these, a white light aft showing all around the horizon. The side lights shall be fitted with screens, to prevent the lights showing across the bow, these screens being not less than 18 inches long for boats of class two and 24 inches long for class three.   Let me remark that the screens alone do not prevent the lights from showing across the bow for a point or so; but a vertical cleat on the forward edge, equal in depth to the distance from screen to center of flame, will prevent the lights from showing across the bow, and should be fitted on all light screens.

The lights specified above are *running lights,* and the circular, under the heading "Regulations," calls attention to the requirement for an anchor light "forward, where it can best be seen, but at a height not exceeding 20 feet above the hull—a white light in a lantern, so constructed as to show a clear, uniform and unbroken light, visible all around the horizon at a distance of at least 1 mile."   The provisions as to lights for pilot and fishing vessels, etc., remain unchanged, and nothing in the act is to conflict with the International Rules.

The circular goes on to require "a whistle or other mechanically operated, sound-producing apparatus capable of producing a blast of two seconds or more in duration," which covers air whistles, electric and mechanical diaphragm horns and similar devices.   Besides the whistle, boats of classes two and three must carry "an efficient fog-horn" and "an efficient bell, which shall be not less than 8 inches across the mouth on board of vessels of class three. The Regulations comment on this as follows: "The word 'efficient' must be taken in its ordinary sense, considered with reference to the object intended by the provisions in which the word appears—the production of certain signals."

Section 5 of the act prescribes "Either life-preservers, or life-belts, or buoyant cushions, or ring-buoys, or other device, to be prescribed by the Secretary of Commerce and Labor, sufficient to sustain afloat every person on board, and so placed as to be readily accessible."

In addition the Department authorizes life-preservers and buoyant cushions for motor boats not carrying passengers for hire under the following conditions: Each life-preserver or buoyant cushion shall be capable of sustaining afloat for a continuous period of twenty-four hours an attached weight so arranged that whether the said weight be submerged or not, there shall be a direct downward gravitation pull upon such life-preserver or cushion of at least 20 pounds. If a buoyant cushion is furnished for more than one person, its capacity must be proportionately greater.

No such life-preservers or buoyant cushions stuffed or filled with granulated cork or other loose granulated material and no pneumatic life-preservers or cushions will be approved.

Planks, gratings, floorings, oars, small boats

in tow, etc., are not approved as substitutes for life-preservers, life-belts, buoyant cushions, or ring-buoys, but wooden life-floats may be used, provided their dimensions shall not be less than 4 feet in length, 14 inches in breadth, 2 inches in thickness, and made of well-seasoned white pine, or of any other wood not exceeding white pine in weight per cubic foot.

Samples of other substitutes for the articles mentioned must first be submitted to the Supervising Inspector General, Steamboat Inspection Service, for examination and approval.

Section 6 provides "that every motor boat and also every vessel propelled by machinery other than steam more than 65 feet in length shall carry ready for immediate use the means of promptly and effectually extinguishing burning gasolene," and the regulations state "no specific means * * * * are prescribed. Besides the usual fire extinguishers, suitable chemicals, or bags of coarse flour or sand, will serve the purpose. All motor boats, irrespective of length, must be so equipped." The inspection department also says that the following fire extinguishers have demonstrated a capacity for extinguishing burning gasolene and are approved by the Department: Alert, Babcock No. 1, Bonner, Childs, Coston, Durkee, Ever Ready, Gold Medal No. 1, Hayward, Keystone, Protector, Pyrene, Paragon, Royal,

Salvage, Stempel, Safety, Success, Underwriters No. 6.

A fire in the bilge, fed by oil and gasolene, is a mighty tough thing to fight, and the ordinary fire extinguisher does not contain nearly enough liquid to subdue it. Preventive measures, such as having the gasolene tanks in a watertight compartment draining overboard, running the pipes outside the hull from tank to motor, lining the bilge with metal under the motor to form an oil-tight pan, etc., are far superior to any extinguishing devices; yet the law, though vague, is mandatory, and such "means of extinguishing burning gasolene" must be carried.

The last regulation, No. 9, is important: "Motor boats are required to have on board two pamphlets of the pilot rules to be observed by them, which will be furnished by local inspectors of steam vessels on request. Copies of this circular should be inserted therein." The pilot rules should be not only on board, but carefully studied and digested.

Dealers in marine supplies can supply the lanterns prescribed by law in the proper sizes for the different classes. Remember that a boat 26 feet long belongs in class two, and one 40 feet long in class three. Brass running lights are more expensive than galvanized ones, but are much neater in appearance when kept polished, though very slovenly looking when allowed to tarnish.

The problem of side lights on a small open launch is a vexing one, as spray is apt to crack the lens and extinguish the light if an oil-burner. The small boat has little freeboard, and the lights are, consequently, close to the water, unless a standing top is fitted, when they can be placed on it. Electric lights are convenient, as they do away with the dirty job of cleaning and filling, and, if care is taken to have all wiring and connections waterproof, are not affected by flying spray or rain. But even if incandescent lamps are fitted, the oil founts should be kept ready in case of trouble with the electric system.

A good whistle—something that will give more than a mere squeak—is a necessity, especially if intending to navigate crowded waters. The average whistle carried on small motor boats can hardly be heard in the traffic of New York harbor, and is really a source of danger, as the pilots of other vessels may be misled by hearing no signal.

In conclusion, let me urge all motor-boat pilots to study the elements of navigation, including compass deviation, plane sailing, finding position by bearings, and the effect of tides and currents. And let them not be content with a mere superficial acquaintance with the

subject, but dig out and understand the under-
lying principles.

Seamanship, also, though an art best learned
by experience afloat in all weathers, yet 'owes
much to theoretical investigation.   Study during the winter, supplemented by practice in
summer, will go far to give confidence in novel
situations.

MOORING EQUIPMENT AND GROUND TACKLE FOR SMALL BOATS.

BY HERBERT L. STONE.

THERE is probably no other part of a boat's equipment on which the safety of the craft depends as much as upon her ground tackle. More yachts are wrecked and damaged during a season through dragging their moorings or anchors in a summer blow than in any other way. The majority of boat owners do not seem to realize the necessity for having a mooring and anchoring equipment of sufficient weight, or, if they have a good equipment, very often they do not look to it that sufficient precautions are taken in properly securing the boat against emergencies before leaving her for any period of time.

This may be due somewhat to the fact that many of the motor boats that are bought to-day, being stock boats, are naturally turned out with little or no equipment. One small anchor is the most that the average builder provides, and the average purchaser is usually content to try to get through the summer without going any deeper into his pocketbook for ground tackle.

This is false economy; for the boat's safety may be many times imperilled in even ordinary summer weather, and the damage it can do to other boats may often be greatly in excess of the damage incurred itself. Not only should every boat owner, no matter how small the craft, see that he has a proper equipment, but he should learn how to handle it, as in no particular is good seamanship more apparent than in the way one comes to or weighs an anchor.

Ground tackle may be divided, in a general way, into two classifications, (1) Moorings, by which is meant a permanent anchorage at which the yacht swings when in the home port, and (2) anchor and cable equipment. We will consider first the former of these classifications.

If a boat is not kept permanently tied to a dock, but is anchored off, or in the stream, as it is sometimes called, it is advisable that permanent moorings be planted, which can be cast off when getting under way and picked up when returning without the necessity of getting an anchor on deck each time. It is imperative that this permanent mooring be secure and plenty heavy enough to hold the boat in any kind of weather, especially where the craft is to be left alone for any length of time.

The weights, or anchors, at the lower end of these moorings may be of varied kinds and of widely divergent forms. In a soft bottom a flat

stone of suitable size and weighing from 150
to 400 pounds, according to the size of the boat,
may be used by drilling a hole through its
center, through which hole an iron rod is run
and fastened on the under side by a nut and
washer, a ring-bolt having been previously
forged in the upper end of the rod to take the
cable. This flat stone will bury itself in the

Mushroom and bulb shank mooring anchor

mud and make a secure mooring, though it is
not as effective on a hard or sandy bottom. This
kind of mooring is not only hard to handle, but
is difficult to take up, and is not as satisfactory
in many ways as the mooring anchors provided
especially for the purpose. The possible saving
in cost of the former is more than outweighed
by the trouble in procuring and making it.

The best form of mooring anchor is probably what is known as the mushroom anchor—
a round cast-iron bowl or saucer, from the
center of which runs a horizontal shank with a
ring at the end in which to fasten the cable.
These mushrooms work their way down into
the mud or bottom, have no stock on which the
chain may become foul, and, when entirely
buried beneath the bottom, the pull exerted is
not only lateral to the plane of the saucer, but
causes it to work deeper into the bottom.

A further development of the mushroom
principle has brought out a bulb-shank mushroom, which has a heavy ball of iron cast on
the end of the shank just under the ring or
shackle. This weight causes the anchor to lie
flat on the bottom at all times, giving the maximum resistance to the strain of the boat, and
prevents the shank from standing upright,
which might be a source of danger to the boat's
bottom if moored in shallow water. Also, in
responding to the jerk of a boat in a seaway
when fetching up suddenly on her cable, this
bulb will rise slightly from the bottom, thus
easing the strain to a great degree.

These mushrooms are set at an angle to the
shank to give the best degree of bite under
strain, and have a sharp edge, which will take
hold in a hard, sandy bottom.

In regard to the size of these mushroom

anchors, it is difficult to make a hard-and-fast rule as to what weight any particular sized boat would require, the character of the bottom and the exposed position of the anchorage being determining factors. Roughly, it may be said that, for a boat under 25 feet in length, from a 75 to 125-pound mushroom would be sufficient in a sheltered anchorage and good holding ground; for a boat from 25 to 30 feet, from 125 to 200 pounds; from 30 to 40 feet, 230 to 300 pounds, and from 40 to 60 feet in good anchorage, a mooring of from 400 to 500 pounds should be sufficient, though, as I said before, a hard bottom or an exposed anchorage would take larger sizes. It is poor economy to risk a vessel worth anywhere from $1,000 to $10,000 by reason of saving a few pounds in the weight of the mooring.

To the ring or shackle in the end of the shank should be fastened a chain cable of ample size, and in length depending upon the amount of room a boat has in which to swing. In a crowded anchorage 50 to 60 feet is all the scope that one boat can be allowed, though more is preferable when it can be had. On the other end of the chain is a shackle with a thimble, around which should be spliced a 6 to 12-foot length of heavy manila cable at least an inch and a half in diameter for boats up to 40 feet long, and from two to two and a half

inches for larger sized vessels. This is to take
aboard the boat and belay over bitts or capstan.
The size of the chain necessary will vary with
the size of the boat; but for boats under 30

Types of mooring buoys

feet, ⅜-inch diameter will be large enough, ½
inch for boats under 40 feet, and ¾ inch for
boats under 60 feet. To prevent this mooring
line from sinking when cast off, it must be

buoyed to a float which may be reached at all times, no matter what the state of the tide. Various types of floats may be used, from a wooden block 18 inches long by 3 inches square to an elaborate can buoy or an 8-foot cedar post with a ring in the end. If a small buoy is used, a light hand line should be spliced through the middle of the hemp mooring, or riding cable (or through the eye splice in the upper end of the mooring line, if finished in this way), and the other end made fast to the buoy. This line may vary in length according to the rise and fall of the tide and the depth of water. It must be long enough to reach the bottom at high water, to prevent the weight of the chain from pulling the buoy under. If a cedar post mooring buoy is used, sufficiently large to float the weight of the chain, the chain may be fastened to it by a ring-bolt and shackle or by an iron strap on the under end of the buoy. A swivel in the chain will prevent the latter from "kinking" as the boat swings around it.

The anchor equipment is no less important than the mooring equipment, and should receive the greatest consideration from the yacht owner, and particularly from the man who is his own captain. There are so many kinds and types of anchors on the market to-day, each possessing its good points, that it is hard to say what type is best, though it is an easy matter to tell what constitutes an efficient equipment for a given type of boat.

For those who may not know the names of the various parts of an anchor it may be well to define them. The shank is the central shaft, from the lower end of which project two curved arms, on the point of each being a broad triangular or half round blade called the fluke, pointed at the outer end. Where the shank joins these curved arms is called the crown. Through a hole in the upper part of the shank passes the stock, at right angles to the shank. This stock may be made of wood or iron, and was formerly rigidly attached to the shank, though to-day in yacht anchors the stock usually has a knob on either end, while one end is curved, the entire stock sliding through a hole in the shank, so that it can be folded back parallel to the shank when not in use. It is kept in position when in use by means of a welded collar and a pin, or forelock, as it is called. In the extreme upper end of the shank is worked a forged iron ring, or else a large open shackle is fastened to it by the pin working through a hole.

In addition to this common form of anchor, a handy and convenient anchor, and one that is coming into more general use on account of the fact that it may be stowed in a small space, is the folding anchor, in which both arms fold up against the shank when not in use, while both ends of the stock fold down against the shank, each being held in place in either the open or the closed position by a pin. These anchors are principally useful on motor boats, where it is not desirable to carry an anchor on deck, as they may be stowed below in a locker or under a cockpit seat, where they may be quickly reached and are yet out of the way.

Then there is the stockless anchor, particularly useful on boats with hawse pipes, as the shank pulls up into the pipe, leaving only the flat flukes protruding. This does away entirely with having to get the anchor on deck at any time.

There is also the grapnel, a small anchor with four or five arms or flukes radiating from a common shank, useful mostly for small boats or as light anchors for fishing or when anchoring for only a short time.

HANDLING GROUND TACKLE.

A man's ability as a seaman is in no way more apparent than in coming to anchor or getting under way, and in the manner in which he handles his ground tackle. Many boat owners who are good sailors so far as handling their craft and steering a course goes, are more or less deficient in the matter of coming to

anchor and getting under way; a fact that is
due, probably, to lack of experience in handling
ground tackle under varying conditions, their
boats riding to a permanent mooring most of
the time, the use of an anchor being confined to
week-end cruises in protected harbors. Especially is this so with power-boat sailors, the
nautical experience of many of them having
been confined to two or three seasons, where
the opportunities to observe and learn have not
always been present.

An adequate ground tackle equipment should
consist of at least two anchors, one of medium
size for ordinary use in protected harbors, and
a very heavy one, capable of holding the boat
in any blow that she is likely to meet. There
should be a separate cable for each of these, the
length depending somewhat upon the depth of
the water where the boat is used, but in any
event they should be at least 200 feet long, and
preferably longer. The comparative merits of
the different types of anchors need not be dis-
cussed here except to say that some shapes are
better adapted to the characteristics of the bottom of certain localities than others, and for
this reason it is usually a good plan to adopt
the style of anchor used by the natives of the
locality in which the boat is kept. For example,
on a sandy bottom an anchor should have long
shank and stock and rather sharp, thin flukes;

while for a mud bottom a short, chunky anchor with broad flukes is best.

The principal qualifications of any anchor are its ability to "bite" quickly, hold firmly, and yet be easily broken out and weighed. For yachts, anchors with portable stocks (the cross-bar near the top of the shank) that are easily stowed, or folding anchors, are in almost universal use, and give excellent satisfaction.

In getting your anchors be sure that you buy galvanized ones, and if a chain cable is used, the chain should be galvanized also, as nothing is so hard on the paint, both of the sides and deck, as an ungalvanized anchor or cable, the rust streaking both in a very short time.

It is impossible to give any hard-and-fast rules as to the proper weight of anchors for a given size of boat, as many elements have to be taken into consideration. A boat with high freeboard and high cabin house or much top-hamper, requires a larger anchor than one with low freeboard and good draft. Displacement alone cannot be taken as a guide, as a deep boat with large displacement will hold on better and cause less pull on the cable than a light draft boat sitting on top of the water, with high top sides offering resistance to the wind. A table giving the approximate size of the cable and anchor necessary for boats up to 90 feet in length is given below. At best these are only

approximate, but they will serve as a guide, and
in every case lean to the side of safety.   On
rivers or sheltered waters somewhat lighter
equipment will suffice, but on open or rough
water it is best to stick to these sizes.   For
general cruising a rule that will suit average
conditions is to allow about a pound and a
half for over-all foot of length for the lighter
anchor for daily use, and from two pounds to
two pounds and a quarter per running foot for
the heavier anchor.   This method of figuring
will be found to be on the safe side, except
where hard bottom is encountered.

		DIAMETER.		ANCHORS.	
		ROPE	CABLE		
LENGTH OF BOAT.		CABLE.	CHAIN.	ORD.	HVY.
Under 30 ft...............		¾	—	40	60
30 ft. to 40 ft............		1	¼	60	80
40 ft. to 50 ft............		1¼	5-16	70	100
50 ft. to 60 ft............		1⅜	⅜	90	120
60 ft. to 70 ft............		1½	½	100	140
70 ft. to 80 ft............		1½	½	120	160
80 ft. to 90 ft............		1¾	⅝	135	180

In addition to the two anchors already mentioned, it is a good plan to have a light kedge
anchor for use when anchoring for a short time
only, or for a stern line when it is desired to
use one; or for keeping the bow or stern from
swinging when lying against a dock or some
other obstruction.   While grapnels may be
carried for light anchors or for mooring the

dinghy, they are not reliable for anchoring and
do not "bite" or hold well.

Position of anchor on bottom before the pull of the cable
turns it over

When an anchor is let go from the bow it
goes down crown first until it strikes the bottom, when it falls on one side with one end of
the stock resting on the bottom. As the vessel
drops astern and the chain pays out, the strain,
pulling on the ring at the end of the shank,
turns the anchor over until the stock lies flat and
the point of one of the arms or flukes "bites"
the bottom, any further strain tending to sink
it further until it gets a good hold. For this
reason it is necessary that the vessel should
have no "way" on it when the anchor is let go,
but should be at a standstill, or dropping back
with the force of the wind and tide. If in a sail

boat, this is always done by bringing the vessel up to the wind until she loses her headway and starts to drop astern, when the anchor is let go and cable paid out.

When the strain comes on the cable the anchor is turned over, and the lower arm bites the bottom

On a power boat this can be more readily done by killing her headway with the reverse gear and, after the hook is let go, giving her a kick astern so that she will take as much cable as is desired, when a turn is taken over the bitts, checking the momentum, and making the anchor bite well.

In a stockless anchor there is no stock and both flukes go to the bottom together. In most of them the shank is pivoted so that the arms, or flukes, swing a certain distance each way, and when the crown strikes bottom the pull of the cable starts to drag the anchor until the points of the arms catch and both flukes bury themselves in the ground. Many yachtsmen like the stockless anchor as there is no stock to foul the cable; but there is still some prejudice against their use by "shell-backs" who do not believe that they have the holding power of the old-style anchor with a round crown and long arms. However, they are coming into such general use on modern steamships, in the navies of the world and even on steel sailing ships that this prejudice seems to be uncalled for. With two anchors of equal weight there are two broad flukes "biting" the bottom on a stockless anchor to one on the old style, though the latter, of course, has the additional friction of the stock lying on the bottom.

In a stockless anchor both arms bite and hold

After anchoring, be sure to give her enough cable. Many boats get into trouble merely because enough scope is not paid out when anchoring. Even in a protected harbor a sharp squall may cause a boat that is riding high out of water to sheer and drag, and unless plenty of cable is down she may go sailing all over the harbor, especially if she drags toward deeper water. If a boat swings badly it is apt to break out the anchor and cause it to drag. This is caused by the strain coming on the cable when it leads off at an angle from the anchor, tending to pull the latter and break out the fluke from the bottom.

A sand anchor, with long, narrow arms and flukes

The length of cable necessary will, of course, depend upon the depth of water, but when anchoring for any length of time, or even for over night, four or five times the depth of water should be paid out, and if it looks as if there would be much wind, something more should be

given her. It is always advisable, when coming
to anchor, to see that everything is ready forward in plenty of time and avoid any danger
of delay or fouling when you have picked out
your berth and rounded to. If you have a chain
cable it is well to range over on deck in three or
four foot lengths the scope you are going to let
go, so that it will run clear. Get the shank
painter off if the anchor is swung forward, or if
the anchor is carried aft get it forward, opened
out and the cable bent on. If the cable is hemp,
see that it is all clear to run, with no bights
crossed and the running part leading from the
top of the coil. In coiling, the smaller bights
should be laid inside the larger ones.

As between a hemp and chain cable there is
much to be said on both sides. A hemp cable
is easier to handle, has more give to it, and
does not weigh as much, while a chain cable
may be stowed in less space, is stronger, and
with a lot of scope, so that the vessel will "ride
to the bight," as it is called, the weight of the
chain eases the strain and jerk on the cable.
The reason for this is that, as the pull on the
chain increases, the curve of the cable is
straightened out, lifting more of it off of the
bottom and forming a long bight, to which the
vessel rides with little strain. If, however, not
enough scope has been given her, a chain cable
makes hard riding, owing to the jerk with which

a vessel is brought up short when she rises to a sea, there being no give to the chain.

I was on a sailing vessel once bound to the West Indies, when we anchored in the lower bay, on account of a S.E. gale. When the wind let up we could not get our anchor for over a day, owing to the fact that the captain was afraid, when he hove her short, that she would snap her cable when she rose on the heavy southeast sea that was rolling on. On the fishing banks, where they ride to a long scope, the fishermen still use a manila cable, on account of the spring there is in the line. A drawback to a manila cable is that, when anchoring regularly on a rough or rocky bottom, the lower end of the cable is apt to chafe or fray on the rocks. In an open launch I would advise a hemp cable for both anchors, while for a cabin boat, if two anchors are carried, it is best to have the lighter one attached to a manila cable, while the heavier one, if it weighs over 60 or 75 pounds, should have a chain cable attached. On chain cables it is well to have a swivel in the chain between the anchor and the chocks or hawse pipe to take care of any kinking in the chain due to the swinging of the vessel around the anchor in the shifting tides or winds, though this is not necessary on sizes less than ⅜ inch in diameter.

When coming into a harbor, especially a

crowded one, pick out your berth and then look to see how the tide and wind serve. If in a sail boat, you will, of course, have to round up into the wind, but if in a power boat make up your mind which will have the most influence on the boat, the wind or the tide. If these are running in the same direction it is, of course, a very simple matter to slow down, round up, give her the reverse motion where your judgment and previous experience tell you how far she will carry, and as soon as she has come to a dead stop, let go and back up as explained before. If you figure that the tide is the strongest (and this can readily be seen by noticing the way the other boats swing) round up head to the tide, and let go in the same manner as before.

Try to pick out a berth that you will be satisfied with, for nothing is more irritating to other vessels anchored near than to have a boat come in, drop her hook and immediately get it up again and hunt for another berth. Also, take lots of room if possible, for any miscalculation in carrying too much way will often result in damage to other boats. Never anchor in the channel and never crowd in and anchor where there is danger of swinging against other boats already anchored.

In laying your cable down below, always see that the "bitter end" is securely made fast so

that if it is ever necessary to let go in a hurry
some time with "way" still on, so as to bring
her up short, you will not lose anchor and cable
in case the man forward forgets to take a turn
on the bitts.   After anchoring be sure that a
sufficient number of turns are taken on the bitt
or samson posts, the last one being a back
turn to prevent any slipping.   If there is a windlass or gypsy forward, two or three turns
should be taken around the drum from the inside out, before the holding turns are taken
over the other arm of the windlass. After making fast, take a range on shore and watch it for
a few minutes to see if you are holding.   In
taking your turns on the bitt, the part of the
cable leading from the anchor must be the low-
est and the other turns taken on top of it, as
otherwise it would jam.   Be sure that the turns
are properly taken on the windlass so that it
may be hove in when weighing without having
to take all the turns off and put them on the
other way.

If it is ever necessary to let go a second
anchor, let it go from the opposite bow.   Pay
out enough cable on the first anchor to allow
some scope to run out on the second, and take
a turn over the bitt with the second cable, letting enough strain come upon it to make the
anchor bite; or heave in on the first cable, let
go second anchor and give scope to both.   If

the boat is dragging on the first anchor, all that
is necessary is to pay out on the second cable,
and wait until the boat has fetched up on second
anchor and caused it to take hold. A boat will
not veer as badly riding with an anchor from
each bow as she will with a single anchor; but
on the other hand, unless there is an equal
amount of scope out on each cable, I do not
think that a boat will hold as well as she will
with two anchors dropped tandem.   This is
done by attaching another anchor on the same
cable and veering away, and is called "backing
out an anchor."   It may sometimes be necessary
to bend on another length of cable to the "bitter
end" in order to get enough scope to prevent
dragging. If it is blowing very hard and you
have a long length of cable out and the boat
is swinging and veering a good deal, it is better
to make the end of the cable fast with a couple
of turns around the mast (if it is a good one)
than to trust all the weight to the bitts or
capstan.   Never put out two anchors so that
the angle between the two cables is more than
30 degrees, and the nearer they are in line the
better.

In lying to an anchor for any length of time
a boat, swinging in a circle with the tide or
wind, will naturally cause her cable to foul on
the anchor stock, if the anchor is one of that
type. In fact, when lying any length of time, a

boat will sometimes get three or four round turns of her cable around the stock and shank of the anchor. For this reason it is advisable when lying at an anchor to weigh at least once a day so as to clear the cable, as it is obvious that the holding power of an anchor is greatly reduced with the cable foul of the stock.

In lying to an anchor for a long time, or in a heavy wind where a boat is veering and swinging badly, the cable should always be parcelled where it goes through the bow chock, or where it may come in contact with a stay or with the stem of the boat. A piece of canvas or bagging makes excellent material for parcelling.

If forced to anchor in a narrow channel where you have not room to swing, or alongside of a dock where you want to keep the boat away from the spiles, it is necessary to use a stern anchor. This may be a smaller anchor, or the kedge, if you have one on board. For this purpose owners should see that their boats are equipped with good cleats or bitts in the stern of the boat, so that they will have something to which to fasten the rode for a stern line. The usual brass cleats that one finds screwed into the deck planking aft are about as much good for this purpose as Fulton's steamboat would be in the international races for the Harmsworth Cup. One should also insist on having adequate bitts forward that go right down to the keelson and are well braced at deck beams, and not trust a brass or galvanized cleat.

In weighing anchor, most of the scope is usually taken in before sail is made or the engine started. It is best to heave in until the cable leads at an angle of about 25 degrees from the bow chock. When this is done, start the engine, if a power boat, first seeing that the steering gear is clear and unlocked, taking the precaution of throwing her hard over one way to hard over the other; also note that the engine is running properly when the clutch is thrown out so that you will not be stopping the minute the anchor is weighed. In a small boat the anchor is usually weighed by hand, and even in one with a windless, slack is taken in by hand until the cable is "up and down." As soon as the man forward calls, "Up and down," break out smartly and haul the anchor up to the hawse pipe or chock. If the anchor comes hard, throwing the engine in on the forward motion will break it out and it can then be hauled up to the chock without stopping the engine, unless the anchor is a big one, and the way of the boat is carrying it aft, in which case the clutch must be thrown out again until the anchor is at the bow.

In a sail boat an anchor can often be "sailed out" if it comes hard, by getting the headsail

on her when the cable is short and letting her fill
and gather way. When she fetches up on the
cable she'll usually start something. On a
sloop or schooner, get the mainsail up before
the cable is "up and down." Then break out
anchor and get headsails on smartly, first seeing
that stops are off and all is clear, and let her
pay off and gather way by trimming in head
sheets.

Sometimes, especially when anchoring on a
rocky bottom, an anchor is apt to get caught or
the fluke wedged under some rock or obstruction, and it will be impossible to get it out. To
prevent this a tripping line is frequently used.
This consists of a small light line fastened to a
ring on the back of the crown, or at the bottom
of the shank, so that the flukes can be lifted out
easily. This tripping line will, of course, lead
through the hawse pipe, or chock, with the
cable, but care must be taken that there is plenty
of slack given it so that there is no danger
from any strain by the boat tripping the anchor.
The tripping line may also be buoyed with a
shorter length, if desired, and brought aboard
when cable is hove short, if necessary. This is
a particularly good plan when anchoring over
rocky bottom.

After getting the anchor up, if it has been
lying in a muddy bottom, wash it off with two
or three pails of water in the draw bucket, or

with a hose if there is a pump aboard.   Do this
before bringing it on deck and getting mud all
over the boat; or let the anchor drag overboard
under the forefoot until clean.   If the anchor
is a folding one or is stowed aft, unshackle the
cable and put it below in its usual place at once.
If a chain cable is used it can be stowed away
in the chain lockers; but if hemp cable is used it
should be coiled down on deck and left to dry
before stowing below.   Never stow a wet cable
below if you can possibly help it as the heat will
make it rot and deteriorate very quickly.

If you have a fish davit forward, and tackle
to fish and cat the anchor, as is the case on most
boats over 50 feet in length where the anchor
may weigh over 80 pounds, the davit must be
swung out, the tackle overhauled, and the fish
hook caught under one of the flukes, or through
the balance link which is often placed in the
center of the shank (especially in stockless anchors) and which will keep the anchor fairly
balanced while hoisting in; then the anchor can
be hoisted on deck easily by one man.

After the anchor is on deck stow it in the
chocks usually provided for that purpose and
lash it fast with the shank painter.   There
should usually be two eyebolts in the deck to
which the shank painter is spliced so that when
it is passed around the anchor and set up there
is no chance of the anchor's working loose.

Fishing an anchor with the fish tackle and balance link

Then overhaul your fish tackle until you get "two blocks" on it, coil down the fall, set up the davit guys and clear up forward.

A chain cable is always made fast to an anchor by a shackle and pin, but with a hemp cable use a fisherman's bend, with two round turns around the shackle in the shank of the anchor and the end passed under both turns and then seized to the standing part, or a half hitch put in. Then it will not jam and can be easily cast off.

Be careful to look your cables over each

A fishermen's bend for making cable fast to anchor

spring when fitting out, and do not hesitate to buy new ones if the chain cables are badly rusted or the hemp cables become rotted or worn. It is best to buy only the galvanized anchors and chain. The extra cost will be more than saved in the additional length of life of both; moreover, an iron anchor and cable are constantly rusting and discoloring the sides of the boat, or the bilge inside.

For a closing word I need only say, in buying your ground tackle get the best, get it heavy enough and get enough of it. Skimp the gold stripe and the easy chairs if need be, but remember that the safety of your craft may often depend on 70 pounds of iron and a few strands of manila, and these want to be of the best.

THE CARE AND HANDLING OF SAILS.

HOW TO TAKE CARE OF YOUR CANVAS SO AS TO GET THE LONGEST LIFE AND GREATEST EFFICIENCY FROM IT. HANDLING AND TRIMMING SAILS. LIGHT SAILS.

BY GEORGE W. ROBINSON.

IT'S the sails that make a boat look "yachty," just as the clothes a man wears add to his appearance. You have seen a Gloucester fishing schooner with a brand-new, clean suit of sails that at a distance you mistook for a yacht; but you never mistook the dirty, "nigger-heeled," square-headed sail of an old working schooner for a yacht.

Some yachts, to be sure, do go around looking exceedingly "shoddy" as to their sails, but you may rest assured their owners look covetously upon the white canvas of the other craft, and would have a new suit if they could.

It is about the care that should be taken of a new suit of sails that I am going to talk to you, and one of the first rules you should learn is to keep your sails clean. With the smoke from chimneys and steamboats and the dust that

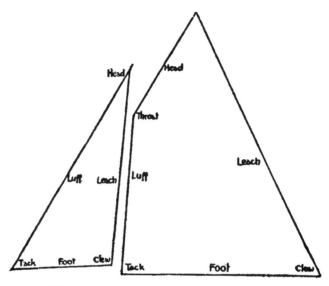

The names of the different parts of a sail

blows from the shore, you will have trouble
enough in keeping a sail white, to say nothing
of the black stain called mildew that is sure
to attack them if they are not kept properly
dried.

Before you open up the bundle containing
your new sails have your decks or cabin top
washed off and dried, for dragging a brand-new
sail over a dusty deck is a piece of carelessness
no good sailor would be guilty of. Canvas will
smut up with dirt so quickly that sail-loft floors
are kept as clean as wax, and the sails are
rolled up in heavy wrapping paper and then

sewed up in old, stout sail cloth before they
leave the loft.

Some amateurs make a great mess of opening
a bundle of sails. Each one of the crew grabs
a corner and begins to pull it into a tangle. The
sailmakers are careful to fold and roll the sail
up neatly, and you will find, if you don't try to
be in too much of a hurry, that you can unfold

The wrong way to lace a sail to a gaff all the weight of the sail hangs on the cringle and wrinkles the sail badly

The right way to lace a sail to a gaff. the lacing is hitched at each grommet hole. distributing the weight of the sail evenly

it in such a way that the head or foot will be
laid out straight. If the foot is on top, roll the
sail over and get at the head, as the part of the
mainsail that laces to the gaff is called.

The shape of the corners should tell you
what part of the sail it is, but for the benefit of
amateurs the sailmakers to-day generally sten-
cil the name on the canvas in black letters, the
peak being the outer end of the head of the sail
at the outer end of the gaff and the throat the
inner end at the jaws of the gaff. The corner
where the boom joins the mast is the tack, be-

cause in old-time boats this was always hauled
tight by a tackle to the deck, called the tack
tackle.   In many old pictures of English cutters
you will see where this tack is hoisted up the
mast, relieving the pressure about equal to one
reef; but on American sloops this tack is generally shackled to an eye or a bale at the goose-
neck, as the iron connection between the boom
and mast is called.   The outer end of the sail
is marked clew.

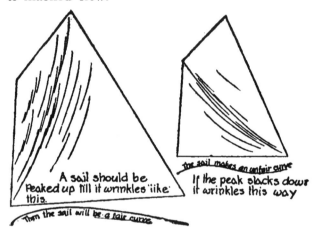

A sail should be
Peaked up till it wrinkles like
this.

the sail makes an unfair curve
If the peak slacks down
it wrinkles this way

Then the sail will be a fair curve

In bending a new mainsail the throat should
be made fast first and then the peak hauled
hand-tight and lashed with either small white
cotton line or, on small yachts, white marlin,
and, on larger ones, small hemp rope.   Some
owners treat their sails as if they were made of
tin instead of a thousand little cotton strings

woven into sail cloth that will stretch, and they pull the head of a new sail all out of shape when they bend it. To prevent this, sailmakers tie a tag to each sail, on which is written the length the sail should be when bent to the gaff and boom. Only one amateur in a hundred will go to the trouble of measuring off this distance carefully unless he is experienced enough to know when a sail is tight enough. The same holds true with the foot of the sail.

When the sail is fast to the outer and inner ends of the gaff, lace the sail to the gaff with small cotton line, not simply passed around and around the spar, but hitched every time it goes through a grommet in the sail. When the gaff is peaked up high, as most modern sails are, this method prevents all the weight of the sail from hanging on the outer cringle, each hitch

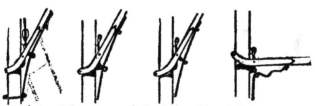

A few of the many ways the throat of a sail is made fast

Shackled to an eyeboll in gaff · Shackled to lower end of tumbler · Shackled to hinged bale in gaff · Slack sail should be left at the throat

holding its proportion of the sail and preventing a lot of wrinkles radiating from the peak. The only objection to such a lacing is the fact that the line is apt to chafe in two and let the

whole head of the sail come adrift from the
gaff. I once won a long-distance yacht race be-

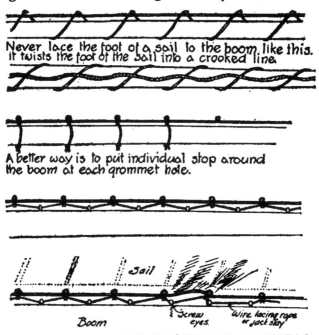

Never lace the foot of a sail to the boom, like this.
It twists the foot of the sail into a crooked line.

A better way is to put individual stop around
the boom at each grommet hole.

Sail

Boom   Screw   Wire lacing rope
        eyes.   or jack stay

The trouble with lacing eyes is as the sail
stretches the grommets and eyes interfere.

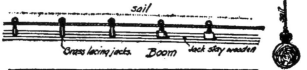

sail

Grass lacing jacks.   Boom   jack stay wooden

A wooden jack stay allows the sail to come and go.

cause the only boat ahead of me had her head
lacing part when she only had a mile more to

go to windward; but with the sail made fast at the two ends of the gaff and his bridles to the peak halyards in towards the middle, his gaff buckled like a coach whip and he had to lower away and relace his sail. By that time we had him licked. To prevent this, it is a good plan to seize the head at each grommet hole to the gaff with white marline, but be sure that your knots don't untie, for white marline is very springy.

Then hoist up the sail until you can seize on each mast hoop, hoisting the sail clear up if it is a calm day; if not, just raise the throat and trice up each hoop as you make it fast, so that you are clear to work on the next one. Then shackle the tack fast to the eyebolt, or bale on the goose-neck, or seize it fast with marline if there is no shackle, haul out on the foot and seize and lace that fast.

There are many different ways in which this lacing that holds the foot of the sail to the boom may be rove; the round and round lacing is wrong, as it tends to twist the sail at each grommet square to the line of the lacing, with the result that the foot of the sail becomes a corrugated surface that extends up a couple of feet or more into the body of the sail above and makes a saw-tooth surface very detrimental to speed. A better way is to put individual stops around the boom at each grommet; these

stops are held in place by opening the strands
of one end and passing the other end through
them so that they cross to opposite sides, and
then around the boom.   This prevents their
falling out when the knots are loosened in
unbending a sail.

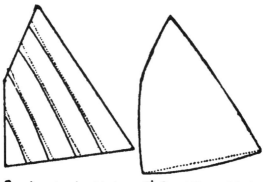

Broadseaming is widening
the seams near the edges to
give fullness to the middle.

The 'roach' in a sail is the·
curve on the edges

A more common practice is to screw a line
of screw eyes along on the top of the boom and
stretch a small wire rope through these and
through small brass grommets seized fast to
the foot of the sail so they all open in a fore-
and-aft line. The only trouble with this method
is that some do not space the grommets in the
boom so as to properly allow for the stretch
of the foot rope, with the result that the sail is
pulled out of shape in one spot by a grommet
in the sail fetching up on an eye in the boom.

The screw eyes should not be put in a new boom until the last thing—not until the sail has been stretched along on the foot and the spots for each marked. Beginning midway between the grommets near the mast, the screw eyes should be spaced farther apart than the grommets are by about what the stretch will be when the sail has been pulled out as far as it will ultimately go.

To prevent all this trouble of possibly scarring up the boom by having to replace the screw eyes, various forms of tracks or slides are used, some of wood and some of metal, with sliding metal hanks not unlike jib hanks in their action, so that they space themselves properly as the sail shrinks or stretches. It makes a very neat-looking rig, and the sail is brought close down to the boom—in some cases too close, for it cuts the knuckles when trying to pass reef points in shortening sail. Another point to be observed in attaching the throat of the sail is to see that enough slack is left so that, as the gaff is peaked up, the rope and sail between the throat cringle and first grommet on the gaff will not be stretched out of shape. Cases have occurred where the rope has been parted by the great leverage the gaff exerts at this corner when the sail has been lashed to one of those patent throat tumblers with an iron rod, into the upper end of which the throat block shackles,

and, into the lower end, the throat of sail. If the
sail is made fast with no slack left when the
gaff lies horizontally (as it generally is when
bending on the head of a sail), when it is
peaked up this distance increases considerably
and is liable to stretch the sail badly.   It is
better to pucker the sail up and have too much
slack when first bending than to have too little.
In fact, when the sail is set the peak should
always be hoisted until the cloth shows wrinkles
running up and down from the peak to the tack
and there is practically no strain on the throat
cringle.

The weight of the sail hangs from the peak
and gaff, and that brings up a consideration of
that spar.   I was about to say of all the spars
on a yacht the gaff is the one you have to be
most particular about, but that would be like
saying the base string of a violin requires the
most attention.   Every string of a violin has
to be in perfect tune, and so it is with a yacht.
Every spar, sail and stay must be set up just
so hard or so slack to properly work in harmony with a certain boat, and just as every
violin has to be individually tuned up to produce
harmony, so every boat has to be "tuned up."

Now, a mainsail hanging its whole weight on
a gaff must be properly supported by the peak
halyards or bridles.   If too much support is
given to the middle of the spar the ends will

bend down, and while the sail through the middle is pulled taut the cloths along the leach are slackened. If the halyards pull on the end of the gaff the outer cloths are pulled too tight and the spar sags down in the middle and slackens the cloths, producing an excessive bag in the middle of the sail. The same principle holds true of the boom, and as every boat has spars of varying stiffness or limberness, and halyards and sheets are rigged in an endless variety of ways, no one, unless he be an experienced man and has the case before him, can say exactly what is the matter with this or that sail.

More sails are spoiled after they leave the sail loft than one imagines. The sailmaker's duty is to use as good a quality of canvas as the owner will pay for, and some firms have made reputations by using only one superior grade of canvas and refusing to make sails of any other stock. Everyone knows what a difference there is in sail cloth—some will pull corner ways like an old dish rag; others hold their shape far better. It is the man who realizes the quality of the sail he has to deal with, and knows by the way his spars bend, and how to rig his gaff, bridles and the pull of his main sheet to make that sail produce the proper curve to push his boat at her best speed, that is classed as the expert boat sailor.

Aeronautics is now teaching many what the proper curve is for the planes of a flying machine, the face of air propellers and the curve that a boat's sail should have to give the best reaction and forward push from the wind's pressure.   Unlike the propeller of a motor boat, that has one speed at which it develops its maximum efficiency, a boat's sail is more on the principle of a reversible propeller where the pitch can be increased or diminished to suit the speed of the wind.

Too many people think that a sail, when once set, needs no attention other than that of pulling in or letting out the sheets; but in that they are sadly in error.   Every change in the wind's velocity requires a corresponding shift in the sail—sweating up to flatten the sail in a hard blow on the wind or slacking down to make the sail more baggy in light airs.   Some people have an idea that a tin sail would be the ideal driving surface, but nothing could be farther from the truth; and often a new, springy, live sail of cloth will make a winner of a boat that has been a persistent loser with an old sail in which all the resiliency has been stretched out of it.

Have you ever seen an aeroplane and noticed the fore and aft curve of its planes?   Well, you most likely saw that the curve was greatest at the entering end and ran nearly flat from the

middle to the back. That, in general, is the
curve we are talking about, and shows that a
sail made with one curve, or the arc of a circle
in its surface, is wrong. The correct shape,
properly described, is a parabolic curve, or a
curve running from the mast in a parabola,
gradually flattening into almost a straight line
near the leach. This may sound complicated,
but it is much simpler than a description of some
curves seen in neglected and misused sails.

Opinions differ greatly as to how much curve
a sail should have and where this draft should
be located, some people going so far as to ad-
vocate a flat, board-like surface for the greatest
driving power under all conditions. This last is
certainly wrong, as one can readily notice on a
light day, when boats with very flat sails are

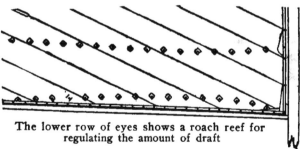

The lower row of eyes shows a roach reef for
regulating the amount of draft

"dead." There is no law to settle the question
as to how much curve or draft to use, and this
is generally left to the experience of the sailmaker. But draft there must be if we are to

obtain the best results. Hence this emphasis upon the importance of shape.

It is up to the yachtsman to preserve this shape by properly hoisting the sail and not hauling it out too hard.

If possible, select a dry, mild day to bend your sail, and when you have it all bent hoist it up not too hard, but properly peaked up, and let it flutter in the wind. This will stretch the sail quite a little and will allow it to be hauled out even more than when first bent. If it is not blowing too hard it would help work the sail into good shape to go out and sail around for an hour or two, but don't, if you can help it take a brand-new sail out in a hard blow, and above all, do not reef it until you have used it a few times, so the sail will not be unduly stretched at any point. In reefing, the outer reef cringle should not be stretched too hard; and yet to be a good sail it must be pulled, so that the cloth when the reef points are knotted lies smooth and flat and does not show corrugations at each nettle. As the sailmakers say, it should only be hauled "hand taut"—that is hand taut when the boat lies at anchor head to the wind; but in actual practice in a breeze of wind you can hook a handy billy or watch tackle onto it and let all hands and the cook of the average lady-handed amateur crew tail on; and with the yacht fogging along, scuppers under

and her decks an angle of 45 degrees, you will
only get that windbag out to an equivalent of
the hand-taut mark of the sailmakers' ideas.
In fact, with amateur crews I generally haul
out the outer cringle first, coaster style, and
then it is far easier to hang on around the mast
and stretch the foot taut by hauling the tack in.
Never sail any length of time with only a few
of the reef points tied down, as it stretches the
sail out of shape; but even if finger nails are
busted and wet knuckles skinned on the jack
stay, keep at it until all the points are tied down.
New skin will grow on knuckles, but the sail

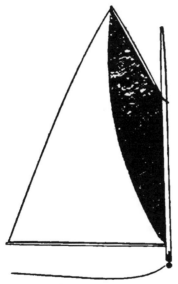

Proper draft is shown by this kind of a shadow

may be permanently bagged by such treatment. When you come to anchor after a day's sailing, it is good for the sail to slack up on the peak and clew, as it allows the sail to come back after the stretching it has received; and as the night dew comes on the sail, by being unlashed, can come and go as the canvas gets wet and dries out.

One can readily see by the shadows on a sail any imperfections in its draft. On a well-setting sail the shadows cut a clean, true curve from peak to tack, more or less rounding, ac-

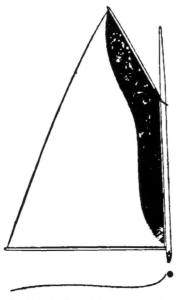

Improper draft is indicated by uneven shadows from **peak** to tack

cording to the fullness or flatness of the sail.
When the peak is not properly hoisted up the
weight of the boom pulls a ridge through the
body of the sail from the throat to the clew,
and the shadow plainly shows up this ridge.

This hard ridge is not as common an evil
now that racing boats have come to the use of
wire rope for halyards, but even with them an
experienced racing man sets his sails and then
goes out and sails around a while before the
starting gun goes for a race. Shortly before
this signal you will see the boat luff up into
the wind and all hands swig up any slack that
may have come with the drying and stretching
of the ropes and canvas.

Racing is a strenuous game, and just as any
athletic sport taxes the endurance of an athlete,
so a yacht race taxes the life of a sail—you
have to stretch it out, you often have to abuse
it by reefing when new, and it takes the best of
care to get a length of life out of such a sail.
All yacht owners are not keen racing men, but
they can take care of their sails just the same.
For instance, there is no excuse for a man's
hoisting up his mainsail where there is a reef
pennant already rove through the cringles, and
letting a bight of this pennant catch under a
cleat on the boom, so that when the peak goes
up the after leach at the cringle is ruined by
the stretching it gets. When the owner wakes

up and slacks off that reef pennant he will find
the after leach so loose as to destroy the usefulness of a good part of the sail.

You have probably seen some yachts on
which the after edge of the sails kept up a constant flutter when the boat was close-hauled,

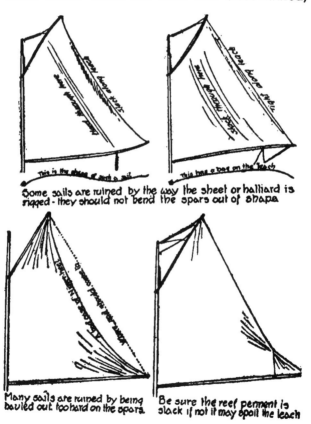

Some sails are ruined by the way the sheet or halliard is
rigged - they should not bend the spars out of shape

Many sails are ruined by being
bauled out too hard on the spars

Be sure the reef pennant is
slack if not it may spoil the leach

and this loose after leach shook the whole sail, so as to destroy half its power. Maybe you have remarked, "What a rotten sail that is!" But what made it so? Oh, the sailmaker, of course —blame him! But only too often the fault does not lie with the man who pushes the sail needle, but with the man who allows his spars to get into a bad condition. I once saw a boat with the main sheet rove in such a way that the end of the boom was held pretty tight and the after cloths were stretched hard; but when the main sheet was trimmed in hard the boom bent up on the end, the gaff end bent down, and so slackened the leach and pulled a hard spot up through the sail over the traveler. The wind went into this sail at the mast, swept in and out again at this hard spot, and there was all the leach fluttering in an uncertain wind.

HEAD SAILS.

The care of head sails is just as important as that of the mainsail. In small boats better care can be taken of the jibs when they can be unbent and stowed below out of the weather. In the old days, when such things as masthead runners were unknown on the old sloops with their tremendously long and heavy bowsprits, the jib was seized fast permanently to jib hanks, which slid up and down the jib stay, and the jib was seldom taken off, but was furled along on top of this immense bowsprit between two small battens and tied down in as tight a roll as her men could stow it with small nettles rove through this batten.   The inboard end was either doubled back on itself or else triced up with a small tripping line from the masthead. With such a rig the jib was always exposed to the weather, and on small yachts, where they had to be left from one Saturday to the next, the jibs deteriorated very fast.   On the larger sloops the jibs could be shaken out, aired and dried every fine day.

With the advent of the cutter rig in this country all this changed.   The cutter set her jib flying, and when it was lowered it was taken in altogether and stowed away below; and when this rig became popular the shape of the sails was copied.   But the Americans would not stand for the jib set flying.   Some of the big crack-a-jack racers and the 40-footers—the class that made the name of Burgess famous—carried jibs set flying in this manner, with wire luff ropes; but the smaller boats carried them on a stay, though not on hanks.   In their place snap hooks were used, so that the sail, when set, had the advantage of the tension on the stay to hold its luff up to windward; and yet the sail could be readily unsnapped and stowed below upon coming to an anchor.   The staysail, too, was set the same way.

Flying jib and balloon jibs had been set this way for some time previous, as it was found to be of great benefit to the pulling power of a head sail to keep its luff as near a straight line as possible. Back stays as well as masthead runners were set up as tight as they could be set by the crew, so as to pull the jib stay and jib topsail stay taut, and more than one topmast was buckled in two by the excessive strain put upon it in trying to straighten the luff of a jib topsail. With this excessive strain put upon the luff of a jib the sailmakers had another problem to contend with. Where well-stretched hemp rope used to be strong enough, nothing but the best quality of steel wire rope would stand when wire halyards and winches were rigged to hoist them.

A jib is apt to "nigger heel" as quickly, if not quicker, than a mainsail, and its life aboard a racing boat is nowhere near as great as a mainsail, for when a sail pulls out of shape to that extent its draft is generally gone. The head and clew generally get pulled out of shape the worst, and to offset this various means are employed. The head is sometimes fitted with a flat board, which also helps to give a greater area to the jib on a given hoist. This board spreader is scored around its edges to take the bolt rope, and is entirely covered with canvas in most cases, some sails being made up with

this spreader made of aluminum instead of
wood.

The clew has a bolt rope with cringle turned
into it and both ends scraped down and relaid,
so that the rope diminishes from, say, ¾ inch
in diameter to a mere cord at the ends. By
gathering in the sail cloth where it is roped, the
two free edges being reinforced with a heavy,

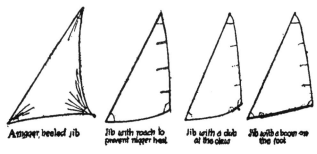

A ragged, heeled jib   Jib with roach to   Jib with a club   Jib with a boom on
prevent nigger heel   at the clew   the foot

wide seam in which a tabeling of wide, flat tape
is sewed fast, the strain is thus evenly distributed around the sail cloth, so that nigger
heeling is prevented. On jib and mainsail
yachts, and, for that matter, on the 90-foot cup
defenders, the strain at the clew, instead of
being all concentrated at one point is distributed
to two or more by clipping off the corner of the
sail at the clew and lashing on a short club.
This is a great help in keeping the jib in shape.
The smaller boats, by having a long club about
three-quarters the length of the foot of the jib,
can so adjust the jib sheet as to make this boom

automatically flatten the jib when hove down
tight on a wind, and yet increase the draft when
the sheet is lifted as the wind comes fair, and,
what is of more importance, it puts the draft in
just the right place up along the stay and keeps
the after edge of the jib flat so the wind flows
off it without resistance against a curled-over
after leach, which throws the wind in against
the mailsail and interferes with the pulling of
that sail.

The modern jib is never reefed as in the days
of the old sloops, where the bonnet was taken
off, as the process of unlacing the lower section of the jib was called, or it was rolled up
and reefed, making an ungainly looking piece
of canvas of the jib.   Instead of that, the
modern racer has a smaller jib, called a No. 2
jib, which is set in place of the regular one
when less head sail is wanted.

It is in changing jibs that sails get the most
abuse, for the amateur sailor has to work under
conditions not generally to his liking, and as
the jib, soaking wet, as a rule, is hauled aboard,
there are chocks, cleats, bitts, etc., for it to catch
on, and it is wonderful how many loops it can
take around various fittings, even to cleats on
the mast, and, finally, just before it is chucked
down the companionway it folds over the end
of the companion slide runway.   Most jibs land
on a dirty cabin floor that may be sloppy with

bilge water, and are trampled on by shoes that
leave a dirt mark with every step. Don't
handle your head sails in this manner! The
fact that most small yachts are short-handed is
generally responsible for such treatment. Roll
the jib up into a ball on the bows and pass it
aft without dragging it as a mop along the deck,
and let another man either stuff it into a sail
bag or stow it securely on a bunk below.

This mishandling of the head sails is most
often apparent in the case of the balloon jib
than any other sail, for in a race it is carried
up to the last minute, and when doused it is
under the bows and in the way from the moment it is not needed. Where it is set flying,
the cleanest way of taking it in is to slack the
halyard only enough to allow a man to unsnap
the tack at the end of the jib and let it fly aft,
to flutter in the lee of the mainsail, and be
hauled right into the cockpit by a man who has
hold of the sheet as the man at the halyard
slacks away.

Where it is lowered down and unsnapped off
the stay by a man on the bowsprit end, he generally has his arms full to smother it, and many
a time it goes over under the bows and gets
away; only to be hauled in, a wet and soggy
mass, over the stern. No man would take a
sail in this way on purpose, but many an ama-

teur can't help it, and it only serves to show what a sail has to stand.

The worst of it is that, after coming in from such a race, many amateurs are so tired that they stow the mainsail and row ashore in haste to get a hot supper, and the sails lay, a sodden mass, in the cabin all night and part of the next day before the owner has time to come and hoist them up to dry. In warm summer nights sail cloth used in that way cannot help becoming steamy and mildewed. On larger boats, where a paid hand is carried, the sails can be hoisted and properly dried as soon as the yacht comes to an anchor.

The shape of the sails and the way the sheets are led are just as important as anything else to the success of a sail, and if the jib is not cut to the proper shape no amount of care on the sailmaker's part can rectify that trouble. A jib should be sheeted so that the foot is pulled a little bit tighter than the after leach, and, therefore, great care has to be exercised to get the lead of the sheets just right. Where a boom is used on the foot of the jib the jib sheet blocks can be shifted forward and aft along that spar to get the strain just where it does the most good, but where the blocks hook into the clew with no boom the fairleaders on deck have to be placed in just the right spot or a loss of power will result.

Jib improperly hoisted
and sheeted.

Jib set properly and
a much more effective
sail.

They should be placed so that the after edge
of the jib lays flat and does not pull the after
edge of the sail in so as to retard the free flow
of air off of its surface after it has given its
pushing power into the hollow along the luff.
Racing sails are cut with so much roach or curve
to their edges that, to make this surplus canvas
lay flat and not curl or flap, canvas pockets are
sewed into the sail and ash battens slipped in
to act as spreaders and keep the cloth flat. Do
not leave them in when you take your jib off.
Untie the strings that close the end and pull
the battens out, or you may punch a hole in the
sail and the constant strain will pull the sail
out of shape.   The same applies to mainsail

battens, and they should be taken out before furling the sail, if possible.

Light sails can accomplish wonders for *any* boat if properly set and handled and there is no good reason why the regular use of ballooners and spinnakers should be confined mainly to the racing craft. It is true that these additional sails make a little extra work and sometimes, with an inexperienced crew, act with some "cussedness," but these things are soon forgotten in the pleasure of the better, snappier and *faster* sailing which results.

HANDLING LIGHT SAILS.

The most common light sails are balloon jibs and spinnakers. These, or a combination sail used for either, are carried by even the smallest racing craft; so let us look at these for the present and leave such things as balloon jib topsails, fisherman's staysails, etc., for some other time.

Whenever possible two spinnakers should be carried—a small one, and one of larger size. Frequently a small, light spinnaker can be used to advantage in airs so light that the big sail will not stay filled out. Then when the breeze comes in, a quick shift, and the large one is giving you the maximum power. In cases where only one is allowed, select a medium size rather than the largest you can carry. This makes a better all-around sail.

Spinnakers should not be made excessively "baggy," as there is certainly no advantage in holding a big pocket of dead air in the sail. It is considered good mechanics to get rid of spent air as quickly as possible, and a ballooner or spinnaker made flat enough to allow the wind to escape is a better sail than the extreme "bag." This is particularly important in the classes restricted to spinnakers only, as the sail then has to be used as a ballooner also.

In stopping light sails, remember the old saying "more haste, less speed." Take enough time, and do it right. If the sail is rolled tightly, it can be tied with less turns of the thread, hoisted more easily, and is less liable to break out before the proper time, or to catch in anything. On the other hand, when you do want to break it, it pulls out with no trouble or swear words. A good way of stopping is to make the head of the sail fast forward to a cleat, haul tight and make tack fast to stern cleat. Bring the clew (sheet) over to the luff (stay). Spread out the sail as flat as possible, and carry the free side over to the luff. Repeat this last until about two feet remain. Then start to roll, as tightly as possible, and put on the ties of No. 3 or No. 4 machine thread. Near the clew two or three turns of thread will be necessary, but near the head and tack one turn is ample. If the luff is marked to show just where the clew should be carried to, the stopping will be correct every time.

Take plenty of time in setting the sail. Nothing is gained by hurried work. If it is blowing, see that the after guy is made fast. Once the sail is drawing, it is a tremendous job to get back a pole that his slipped forward.

A swivel at the head of the sail will usually prevent twisting while being hoisted. If it does twist, however, slack off the halyard about a foot, and the sail will right itself. A snap hook on the tack is a great time saver.

The forward and after pole guys should have snap hooks for quick work. If the forward guy is made long enough, it can be used advantageously in a spinnaker jibe, when it becomes the after guy, or it can also be rove through a bow chock and led aft to the cockpit when "playing" the spinnaker. The halyard should have a snap hook on each end and lead to both sides of the boat. This arrangement often avoids the crossing of halyards, and is generally of great convenience in many ways.

In regard to the handling of spinnakers, it is safe to say that the average yachtsman does not take enough care in keeping them trimmed right *all the time*. On this point of sailing, the main and spinnaker sheets should be played

for every puff and breath of air that con-
descends to blow your way. Don't place too
much reliance upon the fly at the masthead
when running before the wind. It is very er-
ratic, due to draft from the sails, and will often
indicate that a jibe is necessary when the real
breeze is still in its old quarter.

It is a serious mistake to let your sail get in
a bunch or bag forward of your jib stay, as it
retards the speed of the boat, throws her head
off and makes her bury. The spinnaker sheet
should be long enough to come right to the
cockpit and reeve through a leader in the deck.
This makes it convenient to play your sail from
aft where the weight of the crew is more effective, particularly in running off before it. If
you have enough crew, let one man handle the
spinnaker sheet, another the guy and bunched
main sheet parts, while another is on the stick.

The spinnaker may be effectually carried on
the wind in light airs. The jib should be taken
in, as it falls against the light sail and knocks
out the wind. Do not try to trim the sail full
length inside the shrouds, as that would have
a very bad effect, both in itself and on the luff
of the mainsail. Bunch up the clew, pull the
sail into a fairly flat surface, then tie with a
sail stop, and play with a light sheet.

Taking in a spinnaker is ordinarily a simple
matter. Let go the after guy, allowing the pole

to swing forward to the stay, run pole aft, bear away a little, thus blanketing spinnaker, and lower away. If, however, the wind is not dead astern, or you are racing and cannot alter your course, trim in the jib and let it take some of the spinnaker pressure while the pole is being unshipped. The pole will then bring home the spinnaker which was flattened against the jib.

In a good breeze of wind the spinnaker is never effective unless the wind is fairly well aft. One exception to this is when the pole is carried well forward and the spinnaker trimmed by means of the working jib. This scheme moulds the light sail and gives more area. Parts of the sail will flap, of course, but the general result is good.

In most one-design classes the balloon jib is barred, as it usually requires an extra hand on board, and amateur sailormen are comparatively scarce. Hence the necessity for a combination ballooner-spinnaker.

In the regular classes, both sails are used, and there is no question of the advantage derived from spilling the spinnaker into a well-lifted ballooner. This combination can be worked in a number of ways, all with good results.

A well-cut ballooner can often be used in place of the working jib, or backed up with the latter, as described in referring to spinnakers.

In dousing a ballooner which is snapped to the stay, it is necessary to go out on the bowsprit and gather it in as it comes down. With a sail set flying, slack the halyard and sheet enough to enable the man forward to unsnap the tack. If the regular jib has already been set to weather of the ballooner the latter can be lowered and easily gathered in to leeward. If the job is a very difficult one, bear away enough to blanket the sail—then it will flutter down very readily in lee of mainsail.

In racing prepare to take in or set your light sails while still a good distance from the mark. There is nothing gained by hasty work near a turning point. In running, there is a natural tendency to hang on to light sails till the last second. Unless you have a well-drilled crew, *don't do it.* It is far better to lose a few feet running and have everything snug and shipshape for the telling beat to windward.

SOME LIGHT ON THE DINGHY PROBLEM.

POINTS TO BEAR IN MIND WHEN SELECTING A
TENDER FOR YOUR BOAT—CAPACITY AS WELL
AS SEAWORTHINESS AND EASE OF TOWING TO
BE CONSIDERED—POWER TENDERS.

BY F. S. NOCK.

HOW often do we hear the question "What is the most suitable tender for my boat?" And to the man who lacks experience when he purchases a small sailing or motor boat it is really a very serious one. Possibly, in order to obtain such a tender as he requires, he visits one of the motor boat exhibitions or shows, and, although he sees tenders of all kinds, he is not apt to know which is most suited to his requirements. The flat-bottom tender or skiff, large enough to carry two persons on a mill pond where the waters are never ruffled, the dory type of tender that is seaworthy, the pretty little round-bottom boats about 3 feet in width that look very nice in an exhibition hall and are often designated as yacht tenders, the practical rowing tender, and

the power tender suitable for yachts from 40 to
200 feet or more in length, are all shown, and
when the person who wants to purchase a tender suitable for his yacht has looked them all

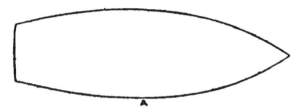

A wide boat with broad stern makes the most suitable
dinghy

over he often finds himself in much the same
predicament as the man who tries to select his
first automobile without having a friend with
him who has been through the game—he sees
so many different types and makes that he is
bewildered. The tender that is suitable for one
person would not meet the demands of another,
and the man who owns an 18-foot boat does not
need the same type of dinghy as the one who
has purchased a 35 or 40-foot craft.

The simplest type of serviceable tender for
general use in connection with a very small boat
is a flat-bottomed affair about 8 feet in length,
with the bottom rounded up forward and aft.
While these are useful for restricted purposes,
there is no need for me to dwell particularly
upon this type, and I will first take up what I

consider to be the most serviceable type of tender which is handy, reliable and cheap; and that

Normal sheer of a dinghy, with bearings carried well aft,
insuring stability and carrying capacity. A good type

is the flat-bottom boat or skiff. They do not
require a great depth of water to float them,
and by reason of this are handy to land in shoal
places.   Another good point in their favor is
that they are easily hauled out on the deck or
in the cockpit of a small boat if it is desired to
carry them, and, if properly handled, they can
be brought through rough water. As tenders
for small yachts, they are very well suited.

One of the greatest drawbacks to this type of
craft as a tender is that the majority of them do
not tow easily or well. But this is not always
the fault of the boat; it can, in many cases, be
accounted for by the location of the fastening
for the towline and the position of the tender in
regard to the larger craft. Sometimes they are
given too long a line, and at other times they
are kept too short. If you want to find out
where your tender tows the easiest, let out on
the painter or towline until the boat is some distance astern and then haul it in until you finally
reach a point where there is very little pull, and

make it fast. Of course, if you have a following sea you cannot haul it up too close, as you
will find that she will be driven up against the
stern with considerable force by the following
waves. You can thus see that the distance at
which a tender should be made fast from the
boat towing will vary with the conditions, and
one will have to learn by experience the best
position for the following boat. If this type of
craft (the flat-bottomed skiff) is towed through
the water at a high rate of speed, it has a tendency to raise the bow and settle at the stern,
and when in such a position tows hard, making
a heavy drag on the towing boat. It is a good
plan to have a strong ring bolt in the stern of
these small skiffs and tow them from that point
instead of the bow, as they not only tow easier
but do not sheer as much.

Skiffs suitable for tenders vary in length
from 9 to 14 feet. In selecting one, take care
that the bottom, at the after end, does not
round up too quickly; nor should you pick out
one that is nearly straight on the bottom. The
sides, whether made in one, two or three
strakes, should have a good flare. And, above
all, do not pick out a narrow craft. The
greatest width of the bottom should not be less
than a quarter of the waterline length. A
properly designed skiff 9 feet in length is
capable of carrying three ordinary-sized persons

in safety, and a 12-foot one should accommodate five or six persons.

The dory type of tender is in reality a smaller edition of the dory, and it is a well-known fact that dories will pass in safety through rough water that would even endanger large vessels; but in such cases you can make up your mind they must be handled by experienced persons. This type of tender has a narrow, flat bottom, and instead of having straight sides with a slight flare like the skiff, their sides are more in the form of an arc, being made up of

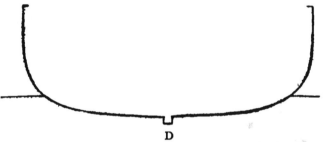

D

Midship section, with good floor and plenty of freeboard

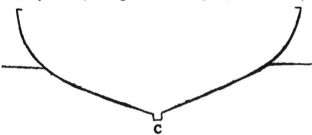

C

Midship section, with too much deadrise and too little freeboard

three or four pieces to a side. They are buoyant, high-sided, tow easily, and, if properly
handled, can be used with safely in very rough
water, but to the uninitiated they often prove a
delusion and a snare. They lack stability, and
when you step into them it is advisable to step
fairly close to the middle, otherwise you may
have a chance to show your friends how well
you are able to swim with your clothes on. I
do not consider them suitable as tenders for
small yachts, except in the hands of experienced
persons; and one should bear in mind that, no
matter how well versed he may be in handling
boats, his friends, especially those of the fair
sex, are not always adepts in the art of getting
into a tender without upsetting it, and if you
want your friends to enjoy themselves, they
must be considered.

Outside of hauling a tender up on the beach
or float, there is nothing built for all-round purposes so suitable as the round-bottom craft,
and I will explain more thoroughly some of the
points that should be considered in purchasing a
boat of this type. When selecting one of these
craft, take one with a good beam or width and
a flat floor, or, in other words, one that is fairly
flat amidships, similar to the section marked C
in the drawing herewith. Do not take a boat
with a midship section (which is at that point
of the boat where it is the widest and deepest)

like D, as such a craft has not a flat floor, and, consequently, little bearing until it is heeled over; whereas C has plenty of bearing, and would not tip to one side or the other as readily. The depth of the boat amidship is another point for consideration. It should be fairly deep (as C), with plenty of freeboard or height above the waterline, and not like the freeboard of section D. The bow and stern should be correspondingly high, to enable one to row such a boat in choppy water without having the small waves slopping aboard. Naturally, it is quite possible for a rowing tender to have too much freeboard; but I can assure you that such craft are in the minority, and the majority of the small round-bottom tenders are much too shallow.

Do not select a tender that is cut away too much aft; it is much better to get something with the bearing carried well aft, as in drawing B, instead of as E. The latter figure shows the line representing the intersection of the garboard, or the plank next the keel, with the keel, and I believe if you study it a trifle you will readily comprehend what I am explaining. The higher this line of intersection at the after end is situated, the less resistance the water presents to prevent it settling when weight is added by a person stepping into it.

The question of a suitable sheer, as the line

representing the upper edge of the boat is called, is difficult to explain to one who is not acquainted with nautical terms, and the best

Garboard raised too high aft to give sufficient bearing.
Sheer and freeboard correct

Sheer too straight, and not enough freeboard forward
and aft

way to describe it is by the illustrations I have drawn of the sheers of two boats. B represents a good normal sheer, with plenty of freeboard or height, at stem, stern and amidship, while F is too straight to be practical or pleasing to the eye.

If you intend to purchase a tender from a builder who is near enough to the water to be able to launch her, you can readily ascertain whether she is able or not. Step into her, and if she is cranky, or easily tipped, don't buy her. A good able 10-foot tender should be sufficiently stiff to admit of the weight of an average man standing on the gunwale or upper edge amidship without upsetting it, and by purchas-

ing something of this description, you will
secure a boat that is suitable, if the other conditions are about as set forth in the foregoing.   A
tender 12 feet or more in length would have
considerably more stability than a smaller craft,
and this would increase in proportion to the
size of the craft, all other things being equal.

Some of you may wonder whether it is best
to purchase a lapstreak, or carvel-built boat.
In the lapstreak tender, the planks lap over
each other—that is to say, the lower edge of
one plank laps over the upper edge of the plank
below—and the carvel-built boat is planked
smooth.   If you intend to carry your tender on
davits, or it is to be kept hauled out on a dock
or float for days at a stretch, the lapstreak tender is more desirable, as it is less apt to leak,
and, for another thing, it can be built of much
lighter material.   The carvel-built boat, if kept
in the sun, or where it is dry, will leak, as the
shrinking of the wood opens the seams, and if
you have a boat of this build hauled out keep
a little water in it to prevent it drying up. Some
of the small round-bottom tenders are built
light and covered with canvas.   This makes
them practically proof against leaks, unless
holes are cut in the canvas, which would not
happen if they are given proper care.   Owing
to the limited space of this article, I cannot go
into the details of construction, but will call

your attention to another type of tender that is
rapidly forging to the front, and not only has
come to stay but offers great possibilities to the
yachtsman in conjunction with his yacht.

The last few years has developed a type of
tender that appeals to the lazy man as well as
the yachtsman and power-boat enthusiast. What
man is there who owns a boat and does not like
to be lazy? That's what he goes boating for!
The tender referred to is the one driven by a
gas engine. These craft vary in length from 10
feet upwards, and are of inestimable value to
the yachtsman. Think of stepping into your
tender and running up rivers and visiting nooks
and coves which are inaccessible to the larger
boat on account of the depth of water! One
can go ashore in the power tender even though
the town be miles away; and on a summer
evening, when there is scarcely a ripple on the
water, one can go with this boat when not able
to sail; and, better still, the owner of a sailing
yacht does not have to depend on the "white
ash" breeze, but by simply making the tender
fast alongside and starting the engine the boat
moves right along through the water. It is a
steady pull and soon counts. Those who have
been brought up with the sailing craft know its
joys and sorrows, and realize how good it is
to be able to make a harbor a few miles away,
when the sun has set and the wind died out,

without going through the laborious work of
sculling the boat in with a sweep, or towing her
in with the rowboat. At the best, this is de-
cidedly hard work; whereas with the power
tender it does not take long to make a harbor
a few miles away.

I have no intention of going into the details
of the power tenders, but I will try to explain
what constitutes a good outfit of this type.
Starting with the small ones, I would state that,
while there are many good power tenders of
about 10 feet in length, the smallest size should
be not less than 11 feet—and preferably larger
if you can handle it conveniently—so as to obtain the best results; that is, to have a power
tender that you can tow properly and, in turn,
can use for towing the large boat if the latter
happens to be a sailing craft. The breadth
should be about the same proportion as the
round-bottom rowing tender, to which I have
already called your attention, as should also
the form of the midship section. The height of
the freeboard at the stem should be a trifle
higher than that called for in the rowing tender; for instance, an 11-foot tender built for
power should be about 2 inches higher at the
stem and a trifle higher amidship and at the
stern. A 12-foot tender could be about 2½
inches higher at the stem; and so on. The freeboard need not be raised a great deal if a nor-

mal power plant is to be installed, but the faster you drive the boat the more need there will be for freeboard to keep out the spray.

The position of the engine is a very important point. If it is too far aft, the boat will set by stern; if too far forward she will not tow well, as she will be down by the head and will sheer from side to side. It should be a trifle forward of the center of the boat, and, by carefully arranging the seats, the accommodations of such a craft would be equal to that of a rowing tender of the same general dimensions, in spite of the fact that you have the additional weight and space taken up by the engine.

Do not try to make a racing boat out of an 11-foot tender. If you put in excess power you can drive them, but only at the expense of having a continual shower bath, which is not usually appreciated either by you or your guests. For an 11-foot tender, an engine that will develop 1½ to 2 horsepower is ample power for all ordinary purposes. A 12-foot tender, 2 to 4 horsepower; a 14-foot tender, 3 to 6 horsepower; a 16-foot tender, 4 to 8 horsepower; and from that size up to 40 feet and over, the power is a factor that can best be determined by the conditions that have to be met. Some of the 20-foot tenders are equipped with engines that will develop as high as 40 horsepower, and I have in mind one 40-foot tender that is fitted

with an engine capable of developing 100 horsepower. Perhaps as I have mentioned the larger
size of tenders, it might be well to state that the
forms of these vary greatly, according to the
conditions for which they are designed; therefore, you can consider that the shapes I mentioned as being most suitable are for small
tenders, 11 to 15 feet in length, and not for the
larger craft.

Omitting the question of anything over 16
feet in length but referring to the average small
tender, one should bear in mind that the engine
bed is so arranged as to bring the strain on such
parts of the hull as will stand it without racking
it to pieces. A couple of pieces of oak set on
the frames is of little or no use. The planking
and frames in the majority of these boats will
give too much to insure the necessary rigidity.
Where the engine is small and light the bed can
be made of a couple of pieces of oak in the
form of floors cut to the shape of the inside of
the skin and securely fastened to same, and to
the keel. The bearers, or fore and aft pieces,
should be cut over these athwartship pieces and
be securely bolted to them. For a light-weight
2 to 5 horsepower engine this is all the bed that
will be required, but if a much larger engine
is to be installed it would be advisable to
make the bed with the fore and aft bearers of
considerable length, and not only cut over the

cross pieces but also skin-fitted and well fastened, so as to distribute the strain over a large area.

Have the shaft lined up accurately, so that there will not be a loss of power through same. Take care of the ignition system, and don't fail to use every precaution to keep flying spray and water away from the coil and batteries. It is an excellent plan to use one of the new waterproof coils, and set same in a box under the seat. The timer should also be protected from spray, and too much care cannot be given this matter. Even with the best of care, the engine on a small power tender has certainly to stand a lot of abuse. The tank should not be too large. These small engines do not consume a lot of gasolene, and the tank can easily be replenished. Too much gasolene, if the tank is in the end, is as detrimental to the boat as adding weight at either end.

SOME HINTS ON TOWING THE DINGHY.

A FEW POINTERS ON HANDLING THE TROUBLE-SOME SMALL BOAT ON CRUISERS UNDER 35 FEET IN LENGTH.

BY HERBERT L. STONE.

THERE is probably nothing that causes the owner of a small cruiser, whether a sail or power boat, as much concern and trouble as the handling of his dinghy or tender while on port-to-port runs, especially when it has to be towed or stowed in the cockpit or on deck, as in the case of most boats under 40 feet in length which cannot carry davits. We all know how "cussed" the little things can act in rough water and in a following sea that threatens to heave 'em aboard with every scend, or makes them take a sheer that nearly capsizes them when they fetch up on the painter.

There is a great difference in the towing qualities of different boats, the models of some being much better adapted for this work than others. Some have a tendency to bury their nose and take a sheer, while others drag considerably or squat on their tail and stick their

nose up in the air when being tower at any kind
of speed. As a rule a round-bottom boat will
tow much better than a flat-bottom skiff, if we
except the dory skiff or a boat with a "V" section forward designed especially for towing.

For a tender to tow properly, she should
always be trimmed by the stern somewhat, and
if she will not tow this way naturally, it is necessary to put a weight, such as a sand bag, large
stone or a spare anchor weighing 30 to 40
pounds in the stern to keep her nose up. Another thing that will help to keep the nose up is
making the painter fast well down on the stem
piece just above the water line, and most boats
built for towing have a ring bolt made fast at
this point on the stem. It is surprising what a
lot of difference in the towing a few inches in
the lead of the painter will make. Watch the
painter well for signs of chafing at the ring
bolt, or where it comes in contact with the
breast hook, if made fast inside the stem piece.

When much towing is going to be done, it
will pay to have a good long painter on the
dinghy, as the distance at which the boat is
towed should vary according to different conditions of wind and sea. In smooth water and at
a uniform speed a boat will tow very much
easier if she is given enough painter to let her
ride on the crest of one of the stern waves
which the boat doing the towing makes. In a

power boat, if the first wave is close under the
counter, she will tow best on the top of the second stern wave, but if you get her back of the
crest of that wave, she will pull much harder
on the painter, owing to the fact that she has
constantly to climb to the crest of that wave.
In a power boat that runs at a uniform rate of
speed, this position is usually the same in
smooth water, and the painter can be marked
accordingly.   In the sail boat, however, the
speed varies and the distance to this following
wave likewise changes so that it will take different lengths of painter for different speeds.   In
a following or bad quartering sea, much more
line must be given the dinghy to keep it from
coming aboard.   In rough water 15 to 20
fathoms is not too much to give her, and the
Gloucester fishermen often tow their seine
boats at the end of a painter two or three times
this length, where they ride much easier.

In a power boat the painter is usually made
fast on the bitts or samson post in the stern
on the midship line, and sail boats frequently
have a leader in the center of the transom
through which to lead the painter.   On sail
boats, however, there are times when a boat
will tow better from one of the quarters than
from the center line.   When close hauled in
any kind of a sea a boat will tow much better
from the lee quarter, while with a beam sea and

on a reach she will do better from the weather quarter. On a power boat, however, where there is practically no leeway the painter may always be made fast on a fore and aft midship line.

No hard-and-fast rules can be laid down on power boats as to the distance at which the tender should be towed. This distance varies with the speed of the boat and with the conditions of the sea, especially with a following sea, which is always the meanest for towing. Always have a painter long enough, however, to give her all the scope she needs, and even then it may be sometimes necessary to bend an extra line to it. In making the painter fast make a hitch that will not jam, so that if you ever want to use the boat in a hurry you can cast her off without any delay or trouble.

It is wonderful how much a well-designed dinghy will stand in the way of rough water. I have seen them ride over a heavy sea half full of water and bury their nose in an oncoming wave until full to the gunwales, and then empty it out over the stern as she heaves over the sea, all the time following along as nicely as can be expected, except for the pull on the painter and the necessary strain on the boat's construction. Such a performance, however, usually causes the tender to leak, owing to the wrenching she receives.

FEELING THE WAY WITH THE LEAD.

BY CHARLES H. HALL.

F OR centuries seamen have been finding the depth of water by the same primitive method of letting down a weight with a line, marked at intervals, attached to it. Where the depth is not over twenty fathoms the weight is comparatively small. For greater depths a heavier weight and stronger line are required. Only in recent years has any mechanical means been used; and we need not consider here the modern sounding-machine, nor the devices for exploring the ocean floors, for they have no place on the small yacht or motor boat, which does not go far off shore.

The hand lead to-day is essentially what it was two thousand years ago, when "about midnight the shipmen deemed that they drew near to some country. And they sounded and found twenty fathoms, and when they had gone a little further, they sounded again and found fifteen fathoms." Whereupon, afraid of a lee shore and being no good on a bowline they "cast out four anchors and wished for the day."

The lead itself is a casting of octagonal sec-

tion with a saucer-like depression in the bottom
and a hole through the top. Through this
hole the line is rove, the neatest method being
to splice an eye in the end of the line, lead this
through the hole in the lead and then pass the
lead through the eye and haul taut. The eye
should be leathered to avoid chafing. The depression in the lower end is to receive tallow,
brown soap or some similar substance to which
particles of the bottom—sand, gravel, shells,
etc.—will adhere. When so prepared the lead
is said to be *armed*.

The line is usually of soft cotton, not too
small in diameter, as it must be handled wet
(and small lines cut the hands), nor large
enough to be clumsy. It should be well stretched
before marking and marked when wet. It may
be stretched by winding it tightly around a tree,
post, or large spar, making the ends fast and
soaking it with water. When dry, take up the
slack, and repeat the operation. Its length
should be checked up at intervals by comparison
with permanent marks, such as brass headed
tacks on the club float, or along the stringpiece
of a dock. The line must be *wet* when compared with the marks. The length may be
measured from the bottom of the lead, but it
is better to measure to the end of the line itself,
and let the length of the lead be that much
margin. The traditional marks are as follows:

At 2 fathoms, two strips of leather.
At 3 fathoms, three strips of leather.
At 5 fathoms, a bit of *white* calico.
At 7 fathoms, a bit of red bunting.
At 10 fathoms, a piece of leather with a hole in it.
At 13 fathoms, same as at 3 (see below).
At 15 fathoms, same as at 5.
At 17 fathoms, same as at 7.
At 20 fathoms, a strand of hard cotton cord with two
        knots tied in it.

The above are known as *marks*, the unmarked fathoms being *deeps*. Sometimes the
thirteen fathom mark is a piece of *blue* serge;
this is the English of it. The marks are all
small, say ¾″ x 2½″, but are quite distinctive
as to color and material, and may be quickly
identified in the dark by *feeling*.

The system of marks was developed for
deep-water ships and is not entirely satisfactory
for light draft vessels such as the average small
yacht. For these the line may be divided in
any convenient way. The traditional marks
may be retained and the intermediate fathoms
marked with bits of cord having appropriate
knots, or the divisions may be in feet. In an
emergency, the depth may be obtained by sounding with an unmarked line and "fathoming it
off" between the hands extended at arm's
length each side of the body. Whatever scheme
is used must be thoroughly learned, so that
there may be no hesitation in reading soundings
even on the darkest night.

The line is usually a little more than ten or

twenty fathoms in length. For the ten fathom
line the seven pound lead is a handy weight,
though for very shallow water a lighter one
will answer. For use on a fast boat in depths
over eight fathoms, the fourteen pounder
should be used. One authority says "com-
mence learning to swing the lead with the seven
pound one, and when you find you can swing
this well, go in for the fourteen pound one, and
mind your head!" This is sound advice and
may save a hard bump. The way to learn is to
practice, and keep on practicing, until accurate
soundings can be got quickly on either side of
the boat. One of the old-time tests of a seaman was to send him into the port chains to
get a cast of the lead, where he would have to
use his left hand. To quote again, "A good
leadsman is not made in a day and it requires
incessant practice for months to be able to
heave out twelve fathoms of straight line, in
the *port* channels, and get an eight fathom cast
properly."

A few minutes spent with a good leadsman
will be more valuable than pages of description,
as example is so much better than precept. A
position should be selected where a clear swing
may be obtained, so this means the weather
side of a sailing yacht. Then there must be
some support for the body as both hands are
occupied. In a sailing yacht stand with one

shoulder against a shroud, or, better, outside
the rigging with a line outside of the body and
secured to the shrouds. A broad canvas breast
band is more comfortable than a line and should
have a lanyard at each end to make fast with.
A canvas apron to keep the legs dry will add to
one's comfort, especially in cool weather, as
the drippings from the wet line soon soak
through trousers and seem to run down inside
of sea boots with great facility. The breast
band must not be too high nor too tight.

The end of the lead line is made fast to a
shroud and the line itself is coiled in the left or
inboard hand, so that it will run out freely and
with no chance of fouling. The leadsman faces
somewhat forward and lowers the lead almost
to the water, holding the line with the right or
outboard hand. A little wooden toggle is often
set into the line and held with the fingers; otherwise a little bight is led between two fingers
and toggled with the thumb. Now the lead is
swung fore and aft like a pendulum, a little
further each time until it gains sufficient velocity. If the boat is moving rapidly and the
water is deep it must be whirled up and over in
a circle two or three times with increasing speed.
At just the proper moment, as it is rising and
moving ahead, the line is released and the lead
flies forward and strikes the water well in ad-
vance of the leadsman's position. The line

slips through the outboard hand and runs
smoothly off the coil as the lead sinks down
through the water to the bottom. The headway of the vessel carries the leadsman ahead
and, if the cast be properly made, he is directly
over the lead when it strikes bottom and the
line is up and down. A quick jerk of the arm,
and bottom may be felt. The nearest mark to
the water's edge is noted and the distance to
the surface estimated. Then the depth is reported and the line hauled in and coiled ready
for the next cast. If in a motor boat haul in
smartly and keep the line clear of the propeller.
There used to be a regular singsong chant for
reporting soundings: this is obsolete but even
now the reports are often "By the mark *five!*"
"By the deep *eight!*", "And a half three," "A
quarter less six," "Mark under water five!"
and so on. The shorter and crisper way is
better, "Two fathoms!" "Three and a half,"
"Five and a quarter." If bottom is not found,
it is reported "No bottom at eight," or whatever length of line is out.

In entering a strange harbor, unless it is well
buoyed and charted, the lead should be kept
going, especially if beating in at night. In this
case the shoaling of the water warns one when
to go about. If in a strange anchorage, a few
soundings around the yacht, taken from the
dinghy, will show whether any hidden dangers

exist into which she might swing when the tide turns. In many inlets, where the current is swift and the nature of the bottom such that it is constantly changing, the lead should be kept going. Continual sounding may look timid, but it is "better to be sure than sorry," and as for shoals, sand spits and such hidden dangers, "better a mile too far than a fathom too near." Indeed, most of the strandings that occur are due to neglect of the lead, the navigator being so sure of his position that he thought sounding unnecessary—until the vessel took the ground.

In running along a channel in a fog it is often better not to try and follow it exactly, but to cross it diagonally. Then when the soundings show that the edge of the channel is near, the helm may be put over with confidence, and the boat run on a long slant for the other side. But if in attempting to run along the center, shoal water is found, it is impossible to tell on which side deep water may lie, and a spoke or two of helm may put her on the flats. Many of us have worked our way up a shallow harbor by standing on one tack until the centreboard scraped, and then coming about amid oyster stakes, have made a leg for the other side of the channel.

Sometimes it is necessary to anchor or heave to and sound out a channel in some obscure harbor. This will be done from the dinghy, noting bearings, ranges and landmarks, and possibly setting a buoy or two, to be recovered later.   But this is seldom necessary on our splendidly charted coast, though it is mighty good practice for the amateur hydrographer.

So much for keeping off bottom—frequent soundings and some head-work. The lead is often a valuable instrument for finding one's position in fog.   For this a single sounding is practically useless, and a series is taken at intervals, with the lead *armed*.   The time, depth, character of bottom, course and patent log reading are noted for each cast of the lead. These are then corrected for the stage of the tide and plotted on a sheet of tracing paper, using the scale of the chart.   A line is drawn for the course (at the proper angle with the meridian), and the point at which each cast was made marked on this line.   Each sounding, reduced to mean low water, is marked on its position, with the character of bottom.   A few meridians are then ruled on the paper and it is laid on the chart in the position found by the dead reckoning.   The soundings on the paper are then compared with those on the chart, and the paper shifted, keeping the meridians parallel to the printed ones, until the proper spot is found.

Any marked change in depth, such as the tail of a shoal or a narrow deep, will fix position quickly, as will a shell deposit or some such feature. It must be remembered, however, that the character of bottom shown on the chart, applies to that spot *only*, and not to the surrounding district. Unless within hearing of a clearly identified fog signal it is well to get an occasional cast as otherwise one may easily be set into shoal water. A large ocean liner grounded on the south shore of Long Island a few months ago. From the course she steered she must have been in shoal water for many miles before she finally took bottom. The weather was thick and the vessel but a few miles to the northward of her proper place, and steering the correct course for the supposed position. A cast of the lead would have revealed the danger at once and a change of course to south would have brought her to deep water in a short time.

Where the bottom has a regular slope and the water shoals gradually and evenly, the depth of water will indicate the distance off shore. Examination of the chart showing the approaches to New York reveals a slope as regular as that of a roof with the exception of the old submerged bed of the Hudson which extends seaward for miles. The depth in fathoms is roughly the distance from the beach in miles: forty fathoms, forty miles. Soundings in such depths, however, are made with the coasting or deep-sea leads, with the vessel hove-to, and need not be considered here.

The Drift Lead is the heavy hand lead let down on bottom with the line made fast with plenty of slack. The lines should be secured well forward, as the bow usually ranges around the anchor less than the stern. If the anchor holds, the line will lead down or directly out to the side. If the anchor drags, the line will tend *forward*. In a warship, as there are plenty of men available, the drift lead is tended. In a yacht it is not, but if there is danger of dragging anchor or parting the cable, there will be some one on deck to keep an eye on things, including the drift lead. At night in bad weather when ranges are not visible, the drift lead will give notice of dragging. It must have plenty of slack line or it may be dragged as the vessel ranges around her anchor.

To sum up: Learn the marks on the lead line thoroughly and practice until you can get accurate soundings quickly on either side of the boat, day or night, fair weather or foul.

Compare the line with fixed marks at regular intervals. Mark and compare with the line wet. Allow for the stage of the tide when trying to fix position. Arm the lead and note time, course, patent log reading, and character of bottom. Soundings on the charts are referred to mean low water.

Don't be ashamed to get a cast of the lead when there is the least doubt as to depth of water. It is startling to see what shoal water we get into when we think we're clear of everything.

Sound frequently in thick weather, even when dead sure you're in deep water. It's good practice, anyway.

Give the drift lead plenty of slack and make it fast well forward.

Keep the lead line—and all other lines—clear of the propeller.

Don't dent the boom with the lead—go to the weather side.

Don't get too near the novice when he's learning to swing—he may extinguish a valuable yachtsman.

THE RULES OF THE ROAD, AND THE REASONS FOR THEM.

A DISCUSSION OF SOME OF THE RULES RELATING TO SAFETY AT SEA. HOW TO ACT IN SOME OF THE SITUATIONS WHICH MAY ARISE WHILE FOLLOWING THEM.

BY CAPTAIN E. T. MORTON.

NOTHING is more important to the safe navigation of the motor boat, especially those of the smaller sizes, than a thorough knowledge and understanding of the Rules of the Road by the skipper or owner. The law says that every boat shall have two copies of the pilot rules on board, and takes it for granted that the owner of a small, unlicensed boat thoroughly understands these rules. While a number of the most frequently used rules are known by amateur skippers, there are probably very few who are thoroughly familiar with all of them and appreciate the various situations which may arise, under even a strict interpretation of them. Some confusion is also caused by the conflict of the international rules with the rules for inland waters, though the waters where each are applicable are clearly defined.

In taking up this subject, it is impossible to discuss all the international and inland Rules of the Road, within the space allowed. Copies of the laws, rules and regulations may be obtained for the asking at any Custom House and at the office of the Local Inspectors of Steam-vessels. The rules are written in plain language and are clear to the minds of those who understand sea terms and usages.

In this country it is the custom for pedestrians and vehicles to keep to their right hand when passing one another. The idea pervading the Rules of the Road is also to keep to the right whenever possible. In nautical language it is called "the law of port helm."

The water is called the great highway between nations, and all ships at sea, in charge of officers licensed by their respective governments, obey the International Rules of the Road. These regulations for the prevention of collisions at sea provide for all cases which may occur in passing, whether meeting, crossing or overtaking one another, without exchanging any signals between ships. Diagrams may be drawn, or small models made to move about, to illustrate all of these different situations, showing when it is the duty of either vessel to keep clear, or to hold her course and speed.

When in bays, harbors and rivers the Inland Rules of the Road are in force; and all ships, large and small (except certain classes of motor boats), must be in charge of a local pilot.

Let an observer stand on the middle of the old Brooklyn Bridge late in the afternoon of any week day and he will see a vast number of vessels on the surface of the river below him moving in every direction, the most congested place being usually between the Battery and Governor's Island. Large passenger steamers appear on their way from North River piers to Long Island Sound. Ships from foreign ports are entering or leaving their docks, being pushed around by busy tugs blocking up one-half the width of the river. Steam-lighters, carfloats, ferryboats and tows of every description mingle in this scene all bound upon their own particular errands.

Every day it is the same, yet not for one minute does it remain the same. All are in

The law of port helm. When two vessels are meeting head on, keep to the right by porting the helm, indicating it by one short blast of the whistle.

motion, gliding past each other with ever-changing positions; whistles tooting, engine-room bells clanging, yet all being carried on with skill and despatch. It is a wonderful picture, this panorama of floating craft, ceaselessly going to and fro; one may well gaze on it with admiration.

In clear weather there is no need of any trouble, if each and every one will obey the rules, answer signals and navigate with due caution. It is a common highway, open to all, with equal rights. Yet many cases occur which the law does not cover directly. The rule does not give a large ship the right of way over a small one, yet when an ocean "greyhound" moves up or down the North River the ferryboats halt on their way and tugboats hurry hither and thither to clear the fairway until the monster ship is passed. Their right of way is understood and recognized, being of such immense length and deep draft that they cannot deviate from their courses. The quicker they are allowed to pass, the sooner ordinary traffic may be resumed.

It is said that "The Rules of Navigation never steered a ship," and the same may be said of the Rules of the Road. They are, however, the basis of an orderly system in force upon the water; their efficiency depends upon their interpretation and practical application.

I will not attempt to give here the entire set of Rules of the Road. It is not necessary, as many of them are so plain as not to need amplification, and are well understood. Such extracts from the Steering and Sailing Rules will, however, be given as are deemed necessary of further explanation to the amateur, with suggestions as to their use.

STEERING AND SAILING RULES.

Preliminary.

Risk of collision can, when circumstances permit, be ascertained by carefully watching the compass bearing of an approaching vessel. If the bearing does not appreciably change, such risk should be deemed to exist.

When crossing vessels are yet several miles distant from one another, the compass bearing is useful to detect any change of bearing. On nearer approach, a more convenient method is to take a range on the other vessel with some object on board, as, for instance, a shroud or backstay, a piece of brass or other mark on the rail. Any place near amidships will serve the pilot to get a range when his vessel is keeping a steady course. If the course is changed, any alteration of bearing would be better shown by the compass.

SAILING VESSELS.

ART. 17. When two sailing vessels are approaching one another, so as to involve risk of collision, one of them shall keep out of the way of the other as follows, namely:

(a) A vessel which is running free shall keep out of the way of a vessel which is close-hauled.

(b) A vessel which is close-hauled on the port tack shall keep out of the way of a vessel which is close-hauled on the starboard tack.

(c) When both are running free, with the wind on different sides, the vessel which has the wind on the port side shall keep out of the way of the other.

(d) When both are running free, with the wind on the same side, the vessel which is to the windward shall keep out of the way of the vessel which is to the leeward.

(e) A vessel which has the wind aft shall keep out of the way of the other vessel.

By this rule, a vessel sailing by the wind on the starboard tack (that is, with the wind on the starboard side) has the right of way over all other vessels under way. A vessel on the port tack must keep out of the way of a vessel on the starboard tack, keeping off and passing astern of her, if necessary. Yet a vessel close-hauled on the port tack has the right of way over one which is running free. A vessel which has the wind aft shall keep out of the way of all other vessels under sail.

When two vessels cross courses on different tacks, the old rule of keeping to the right is evident. At night the vessel on the port tack would see to leeward (that is, on her own starboard side) the red light of the vessel on the starboard tack, opposed to her own green light. The vessel on the port tack must port her helm; that is, keep off to the right hand, show her red light to the other vessel and pass astern of her.

STEAM VESSELS.

ART. 18. RULE I. When steam vessels are approaching each other head and head, that is, end on, or nearly so, it shall be the duty of each to pass on the port side of the other; and either vessel shall give, as a signal of her intention, one short and distinct blast of her whistle, and thereupon such vessels shall pass on the port side of each other. But if the courses of such vessels are so far on the starboard of each other as not to be considered as meeting head and head, either vessel shall immediately give two short and distinct blasts of her whistle, which the other vessel shall answer promptly by two similar blasts of her whistle, and they shall pass on the starboard side of each other.

The foregoing only applies to cases where vessels are meeting end on, or nearly end on, in such a manner as to involve risk of collision; in other words, to cases in which, by day, each vessel sees the masts of the other in a line, or nearly in a line, with her own, and by night to cases in which each vessel is in such a position as to see both the sidelights of the other.

It does not apply by day to cases in which a vessel sees another ahead crossing her own course, or by night to cases where the red light of one vessel is opposed to the red light of the other, or where the green light of one vessel is opposed to the green light of the other, or where a red light without a green light or a green light without a red light, is seen ahead, or where both green and red lights are seen anywhere but ahead.

Here is the old law of port helm again. Beginners are often confused by the way the terms "port" and "starboard" are used in handling the *wheel*. When the *helm* is put to port, the *wheel* is turned away from the port and toward the starboard side. The vessel's head is also turned toward the starboard side as it swings in the same direction as the top of the wheel.

This statement needs a modification, as there are exceptions to it. Most steering gears are rove so that the vessel's head moves *with* or in the same direction as the wheel, though many river boats, New York tow-boats, as well as other small steamers and many motor boats have their steering gear rove off so that the wheel moves in a contrary way to the head.

Where the head moves contrary to the wheel, it reminds one of prying on a lever. In steering with a tiller, it is pushed in an opposite way to the rudder and the vessel's head, yet it does not cause any such confusion as a wheel with the gear reversed. These different customs are of long standing and seem likely to continue.

At night, in passing on a port helm, each vessel sees the red light of the other. If passing green to green, strict watch must be kept that the approaching vessel does not port and show her red light, as often happens. This is one reason why it is best to blow a signal and receive a proper answer, as it will remove any doubt as to the intentions of both vessels.

When some distance away, or when a strong wind is blowing, the escaping steam from an approaching steamer's whistle is often seen to indicate one or two blasts, when no sound is heard.

Steam often condenses in the steam pipe leading to the whistle. In an attempt to blow a signal, water and steam escape, making no sound. If then the whistle-cord is relaxed and pulled again to sound a blast, it may appear from a distance like a two-blast signal, while only one is intended or really sounded.

RULE III. If, when steam vessels are approaching each other, either vessel fails to understand the course or intention of the other, from any cause, the vessel so in doubt shall immediately signify the same by giving several short and rapid blasts, not less than four, of the steam whistle.

This rule for inland waters has been amended by the Supervising Inspectors to read:

RULE I. If, when steam vessels are approaching each other, either vessel fails to understand the course or intention of the other, from any cause, the vessel so in doubt shall immediately signify the same by giving several short and rapid blasts, not less than four, of the steam whistle, the danger signal.

Whenever the danger signal is given, the engines of both steamers shall be stopped and backed until the headway of the steamers has been fully checked; nor shall the engines of either steamer be again started ahead until the steamers can safely pass each other, and the proper signals for passing have been given, answered, and understood.

RULE II. Steam vessels are forbidden to use what has become technically known among pilots as "cross signals," that is, answering one whistle with two, and answering two whistles with one. In all cases, and under all circumstances, a pilot receiving either of the whistle signals provided in the rules, which for any reason he deems injudicious to comply with, instead of answering it with a cross signal, shall at once sound the danger signal and observe the rule applying thereto (Rule I).

Much controversy is held over these two rules; no others are so frequently violated. It is a good rule that makes it unlawful to disregard proper signals; nevertheless they cannot always be strictly followed. Many propeller boats will swing around across channel as soon as the engines are worked astern. This renders them without control by the helm. Other vessels approaching or following may be forced to check their way by stopping or backing, causing them similar difficulties.

In crowded waters where cross signals are frequently heard, the excuse can be made that they were intended for another vessel.

RULE VIII. When steam vessels are running in the same direction, and the vessel which is astern shall desire to pass on the right or starboard hand of the vessel ahead, she shall give one short blast of the steam whistle, as a signal of such desire, and if the vessel ahead answers with one blast, she shall put her helm to port; or if she shall desire to pass on the left or port side of the vessel ahead, she shall give two short blasts of the steam whistle as a signal of such desire, and if the vessel ahead answers with two blasts, shall put her helm to starboard; or if the vessel ahead does not think it safe for the vessel astern to attempt to pass at that point, she shall immediately signify the same by giving several short and rapid blasts of the steam whistle, not less than four, and under no circumstances shall the vessel astern attempt to pass the vessel ahead until such time as they have reached a point where it can be safely done, when said vessel ahead shall signify her willingness by blowing the proper signals. The vessel ahead shall in no case attempt to cross the bow or crowd upon the course of the passing vessel.

The signal of one blast signifies a port helm and two blasts a starboard helm when given by an overtaking steamer. The answer is merely an assent to the overtaking steamer's adopting that course. This rule has been both abused and disregarded, especially by a steamer which may have an object in keeping ahead of another independent of the question of safety in passing. Oblique courses are steered across rivers or channels to prevent rival steamers from passing. Both steamers, in such a case, disobey the rule; one by making an attempt to pass without the proper signals, and the other by purposely crowding upon her course.

RULE IX. The whistle signals provided in the rules under this article, for steam vessels meeting, passing, or overtaking, are never to be used except when steamers are in sight of each other, and the course and position of each can be determined in the daytime by a sight of the vessel itself or by night, by seeing its signal lights. In fog, mist, falling snow or heavy rainstorms, when vessels cannot see each other, fog signals only must be given.

Exceptions have been taken to this rule, and steamers have frequently crept by each other during a dense fog, without mishap, by giving passing signals. However, the law could not sanction any such procedure and those who practice it must do so at their own risk.

TWO STEAM VESSELS CROSSING.

ART. 19.   When two steam vessels are crossing, so as to involve risk of collision, the vessel which has the other on her own starboard side shall keep out of the way of the other.

We recognize the law of port helm here again.   The vessel having the other on her own starboard side must watch the approaching vessel, and if any doubt exists about being able to pass ahead of her in perfect safety the wheel should be ported to swing off and pass under her stern.

If dangerously close, and too late to swing off under the other vessel's stern, starboard the wheel to pass clear ahead of her.   If necessary, slow, stop or back the engines.

STEAM VESSEL SHALL KEEP OUT OF THE WAY OF SAILING VESSEL.

ART. 20.   When a steam vessel and a sailing vessel are proceeding in such directions as to involve risk of collision, the steam vessel shall keep out of the way of the sailing vessel.

COURSE AND SPEED.

ART. 21.   Where, by any of these rules, one of the two vessels is to keep out of the way, the other shall keep her course and speed.

As sailing vessels depend altogether upon the direction and force of the wind to move them, it is properly the duty of steam vessels to keep out of their way. Nevertheless, due regard should be shown to the difficulties which may beset either vessel. Circumstances are sometimes such that it is nearly impossible for a steamer to clear herself, while the sailing vessel can sheer off easily.

Tacking ship and altering courses in the way of steamers is extremely dangerous and to be avoided whenever possible.

CROSSING AHEAD.

ART. 22. Every vessel which is directed by these rules to keep out of the way of another vessel shall, if the circumstances of the case admit, avoid crossing ahead of the other.

STEAM VESSEL SHALL SLACKEN SPEED OR STOP.

ART. 23. Every steam vessel which is directed by these rules to keep out of the way of another vessel shall, on approaching her, if necessary, slacken her speed or stop or reverse.

These rules are precautionary and should be followed closely whenever necessity arises.

OVERTAKING VESSELS.

ART. 24. Notwithstanding anything contained in these rules every vessel, overtaking

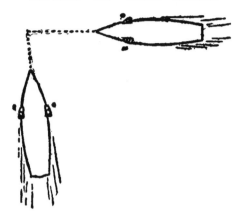

From Rule 19. The upper vessel, having the other on her own port side, has the right of way in crossing.

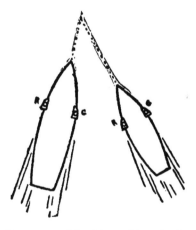

In overtaking a vessel in this position, the foregoing rule and Rule 24 are apt to be confused. The vessel on the right is the overtaking vessel, but when she reaches this position she has the other on her own port hand, and may try to claim that she is a crossing vessel. She is, however, an overtaking vessel until clear.

any other, shall keep out of the way of the
overtaken vessel.

Every vessel coming up with another vessel
from any direction more than two points abaft
her beam, that is, in such a position, with reference to the vessel which she is overtaking, that
at night she would be unable to see either of
that vessel's sidelights, shall be deemed to be an
overtaking vessel; and no subsequent alteration
of the bearing between the two vessels shall
make the overtaking vessel a crossing vessel
within the meaning of these rules, or relieve
her of the duty of keeping clear of the overtaken vessel until she is finally past and clear.

As by day the overtaking vessel cannot always know with certainty whether she is forward of or abaft this direction from the other
vessel she should, if in doubt, assume that she
is an overtaking vessel and keep out of the
way.

Fast sailing vessels, when conditions favor
them, may overtake steam vessels of low power.
Overtaking vessels must keep out of the way
of those overtaken in this case, as with other
vessels.

When one vessel passes another and both are
steering nearly the same course, the former is,
without question by either vessel, regarded as
an overtaking vessel.   When overtaking at a

large angle and passing another on her own port side, she is likely to consider herself a crossing vessel; and, as she shows her red light to the other, will claim the right of way. The other vessel, confident the first is overtaking her, holds her course and speed as the law directs. Under such circumstances, it frequently happens that two vessels approach each other dangerously close, before either or both alter their courses.

In overtaking a vessel on the port quarter, the case is a simple one; as the faster vessel, showing her green light to the other, whether overtaking or crossing, would be obliged to keep clear of the other.

NARROW CHANNELS.

ART. 25. In narrow channels every steam vessel shall, when it is safe and practicable, keep to that side of the fairway or mid-channel which lies on the starboard side of such vessel.

RIGHT OF WAY OF FISHING VESSELS.

ART. 26. Sailing vessels under way shall keep out of the way of sailing vessels or boats fishing with nets, or lines, or trawls. This rule shall not give to any vessel or boat engaged in fishing the right of obstructing a fairway used by vessels other than fishing vessels or boats.

In Article 25 we have again the law of port
helm, keeping to the right hand, to be used
when safe and practicable.

GENERAL PRUDENTIAL RULE.

ART. 27.   In obeying and construing these
rules due regard shall be had to all dangers of
navigation and collision, and to any special circumstances which may render a departure from
the above rules necessary in order to avoid
immediate danger.

No fixed rules can be made to regulate every
signal and movement when danger is imminent.
Collisions must be avoided by whatever means
possible when the rules are not adequate or
effective.   Safety will depend upon good judgment and quick action by both vessels.   When a
collision is impending, endeavor to swing vessels so as to strike a glancing rather than a head
on blow.   Above all things, strive not to present
the broadside to the bow of the other vessel.

One should be extremely cautious how he de-
parts from the rules, yet there are times when
it is not only permissible but imperative to over-
step all rules.

ART. 28.   When vessels are in sight of one
another a steam vessel under way whose engines are going at full speed astern shall indi-

cate that fact by three short blasts on the whistle.

In this situation, two steamers are approaching each other at right angles, or obliquely, *without involving risk of collision,* the course and speed of both being such as would allow the steamer having the other on own starboard side to cross the bow of the other without interfering with the course and speed of the other. In this case the steamer having the other on own *starboard* side may cross ahead of the other, after giving the necessary signals, and receiving the assent of the other steamer.

PRECAUTION.

ART. 29. Nothing in these rules shall exonerate any vessel, or the owner or master or crew thereof, from the consequences of any neglect to carry lights or signals, or of any neglect to keep a proper lookout, or of the neglect of any precaution which may be required by the ordinary practice of seamen, or by the special circumstances of the case.

A steamer's masthead light or other white

light forward is easily seen at a distance. If range lights are used the angle of the steamer's course can be judged by them without seeing the sidelights. Sailing vessels should keep a good watch that their sidelights are kept burning. They should keep a torch or flare-up light ever ready to exhibit in case their sidelights are not noticed, and to show over the stern to overtaking vessels.

A skillful helmsman at the wheel and a lookout forward are requisite even on motor boats and especially in crowded waters. Entering port or when a fog shuts in, the engineers must be notified to "stand by."

A lead and line for sounding are often needed quickly. Oil lights must be provided in case the electric lights are extinguished from any cause. An anchor should be ready for use, with men stationed to handle it promptly when ordered.

STEAM VESSELS—RANGE LIGHTS.

(e) A sea-going steam vessel, when under way, may carry an additional white light similar in construction to the light mentioned in subdivision (a). These two lights shall be so placed in line with the keel that one shall be at least fifteen feet higher than the other, and in such a position with reference to each other that the lower light shall be forward of the upper one.   The vertical distance between these lights shall be less than the horizontal distance.

(f) All steam vessels (except sea-going vessels and ferryboats) shall carry in addition to green and red lights required by article two (b), (c), and screens as required by article two (d), a central range of two white lights; the after light being carried at an elevation at least fifteen feet above the light at the head of the vessel.   The headlight shall be so constructed as to show an unbroken light through twenty points of the compass, namely, from right ahead to two points abaft the beam on either side of the vessel, and the after light so as to show all around the horizon.

Here it is made optional with sea-going steam vessels whether they carry a range light aft or not.   If carried, it must be a white light of similar construction to the forward masthead light.   According to these rules there is no fixed light provided to show astern.

All steam vessels *except* sea-going vessels must carry range lights, the after light to show all around the horizon.   When the range lights of a steamer are seen exactly in line, they may appear like the lights of a towing steamer when at a distance.   When opened out, and the light aft is at a proper height, they are a good guide to show at what angle the vessel is approaching before the sidelights can be seen. It sometimes happens that the after range light is so near on a level with the forward light that one cannot be distinguished from the other; and their usefulness is consequently destroyed. However, two lights are better than one, for if one becomes dim the other may be seen.

LIGHTS FOR AN OVERTAKEN VESSEL.

ART. 10. A vessel which is being overtaken by another, except a steam vessel with an after range light showing all around the horizon, shall show from her stern to such last-mentioned vessel a white light or a flare-up light.

This rule is made for vessels not carrying an after range light visible all around the horizon. With a range light aft showing all around the horizon, another white light shown at the stern below would be confusing, as it would appear like the range lights of a vessel coming head on.

By the International Rules, the range light aft, which may be carried, cannot be seen over two points abaft the beam on either side. A provision is made in the rules whereby a fixed light may be carried astern, but it is not compulsory. It is as follows:

LIGHTS FOR AN OVERTAKEN VESSEL.

ART. 10. A vessel which is being overtaken by another shall show from her stern to such last-mentioned vessel a white light or a flare-up light.

The white light required to be shown by this article may be fixed and carried in a lantern, but in such case the lantern shall be so constructed, fitted, and screened that it shall throw an unbroken light over an arc of the horizon of twelve points of the compass, namely, for six points from right aft on each side of the vessel, so as to be visible at a distance of at least one mile. Such light shall be carried as nearly as practicable on the same level as the side lights.

INLAND RULES.

STEAM VESSEL UNDER WAY (IN A FOG).

(a) A steam vessel under way shall sound, at intervals of not more than one minute, a prolonged blast.

INTERNATIONAL RULES.

STEAM VESSEL UNDER WAY (IN A FOG).

(a) A steam vessel having way upon her shall sound, at intervals of not more than two minutes, a prolonged blast.

(b) A steam vessel under way, but stopped, and having no way upon her, shall sound, at intervals of not more than two minutes, two prolonged blasts, with an interval of about one second between.

A difference is noticed here in the interval allowed between signals sounded in a fog for inland waters and at sea. Two minutes is too long an interval for fast moving steamers.

The signal for a vessel stopped is not provided in the Inland Rules. The International Rule is very useful for vessels arriving near the mouth of rivers and harbors, especially when picking up pilots or discharging them. Again, when two vessels meet dangerously close together, if one is known to be stopped the other can feel her way safely past her.

When running in a dense fog, the best time and courses can be made by going full speed, yet it is in violation of the rules; and, in case of accident, the offender must bear the consequences. Some insist on anchoring, if they can get bottom, as soon as a fog shuts in, but this does not ensure safety. It is not right to anchor in a main ship channel, or narrow passage where there is constant traffic. A vessel under way often has the advantage of being able to move from a place of danger.

Above all, when in the confusion of traffic

around our busiest seaports, be prompt in giving and answering signals, keep a lookout for ferryboats leaving their slips and especially for large steamers backing out of their docks.

The following familiar verses are easily committed to memory and a great aid in keeping the rules in mind:

"Meeting steamers do not dread
When you see three lights ahead,
Port your helm and show your red.

Green to green, or red to red,
Perfect safety, go ahead.

If to starboard red appear
'Tis your duty to keep clear;
To act as judgment says is proper,
Port, or starboard, back or stop her.
But when upon your port is seen
A steamer's starboard light of green,
There's not so much for you to do,
For green to port keeps clear of you.

Both in safety and in doubt,
Always keep a good lookout;
In danger with no room to turn,
Ease her, stop her, go astern."

THE COMPASS.

DESCRIPTION. VARIATION AND DEVIATION AND
HOW THEY ARE APPLIED

BY C. S. STANWORTH,

Commander U. S. Navy, Retired.

THE mariner's compass consists of a single magnet, or, more usually, a series of magnets attached to a graduated card, pivoted at the center and revolving freely in the horizontal plane, the earth's directive force constraining the magnets to lie in the magnetic meridian. To lessen the vibrations, the magnets are generally arranged in pairs, on either side of the North-South line of the card, and since a wire can be more uniformly magnetized, the magnets are composed of bundles of wire bound together.

The circular card is graduated around the periphery into thirty-two divisions of eleven and one-quarter degres each, called points, and these are further subdivided into one-quarter and one-half points.

In addition, the card is graduated into degrees reading from zero to 90 degrees from North to East, North to West, South to East, and South to West. An effort is now being made to introduce a card, graduated from 0 degrees at North, entirely around to 359 degrees by way of East.

BOXING THE COMPASS.

This is naming the points in their regular order and should be learned by all yachtsmen.

Compass card, showing two methods of numbering the degrees

North, South, East and West are called the cardinal points, and N. E., N. W., S. E., S. W.

lying midway between are the inter-cardinal points. The following table gives the names of the points and fractional points:

BOXING THE COMPASS.

North.	East.
N. ½ E.	E. ½ S.
N. x E.	E. x S.
N. x E. ½ E.	E. S. E. ½ E.
N. N. E.	E. S. E.
N. N. E. ½ E.	S. E. x E. ½ E.
N. E. x N.	S. E. x E.
N. E. ½ N.	S. E. ½ E.
N. E.	S. E.
N. E. ½ E.	S. E. ½ S.
N. E. x E.	S. E. x S.
N. E. x E. ½ E	S. S. E. ½ E.
E. N. E.	S. S. E.
E. N. E. ½ E.	S. x E. ½ E.
E. x N.	S. x E.
E. ½ N.	S. ½ E.

South.	West.
S. ½ W.	W. ½ N.
S. x W.	W. x N.
S. x W. ½ W.	W. N. W. ½ W.
S. S. W.	W. N. W.
S. S. W. ½ W.	N. W. x W. ½ W.
S. W. x S.	N. W. x W.
S. W. ½ S.	N. W. ½ W.
S. W.	N. W.
S. W. ½ W.	N. W. ½ N.
S. W. x W.	N. W. x N.
S. W. x W. ½ W.	N. N. W. ½ W.
W. S. W.	N. N. W.
W. S. W. ½ W.	N. x W. ½ W.
W. x S.	N. x W.
W. ½ S.	N. ½ W.

The compass card is mounted in a heavily weighted bowl, carried on gimbals, allowing the card to remain horizontal during rolling and pitching of the ship. A vertical line called the lubber's line is marked on the inner surface of the bowl, and the compass must be so placed that the line from the center of compass card to the lubber's line is parallel to the ship's keel, in order that the lubber's line will indicate the compass direction of the ship's head.

LIQUID COMPASS.

There are two varieties of mariner's compasses, liquid and dry. The U. S. Navy liquid compass is a skeleton card of tinned brass, resting on a central pivot, and partly floating in a liquid composed of nearly equal parts of alcohol and water, a mixture that will remain liquid with a temperature as low as —10 degrees F.

The magnets consist of four bundles of steel wires in sealed cylindrical cases secured to the card, parallel to the North-South line, one pair along the chords 15 degrees from North, the other along the chords 45 degrees from North. The entire card weighs about 3,000 grains, but it is partly buoyed by a spheroidal air vessel, so that the weight resting on the pivot is about 75 grains. The card is contained in a cast bronze bowl, fitted with an elastic metal air chamber, that takes up the variations of volume in the liquid caused by changes in temperature and prevents the formation of air bubbles.

AZIMUTH CIRCLE.

The rim of the compass bowl is turned true,
and fitting loosely over it is a copper ring carrying sight vanes. By sighting through the vanes,
revolving the ring—called an azimuth circle—
until the line of sight passes through any object,
the compass bearing of the object can be obtained. The azimuth circle is generally fitted
with shade glasses, so that bearings of the sun
can be obtained, and also with a mirror that
reflects the sun's rays in a vertical pencil of
light, giving the bearing or azimuth of the sun.

DRY COMPASS.

In a dry compass the magnets and card are
supported by a fine pivot or needle in the center,
the whole being nicely balanced, but not being
supported by any liquid in the compass bowl.
This results in an unsteady card that swings
violently and quickly with the motion of a boat,
and takes some time to steady.

The Lord Kelvin dry compass is a strong
paper card, with its center cut out and rim
stiffened by a light aluminum ring. The pivot
is fitted with an iridium point, on which rests an
aluminum boss. Radiating from this boss are
thirty-two silk threads made fast to the inner
edge of the card, these threads carrying the
weight of the card, and absorbing sudden

shocks. Eight small steel wire needles are normally secured to two silk threads parallel to the East-West line, and are slung from the aluminum ring by other threads, the needles being below the radial threads to lower the center of gravity.

BINNACLES.

Most compasses are mounted in stands called binnacles, and these may be either compensating or non-compensating. The compensating binnacles are arranged with trays of magnets to compensate for any deviation of the compass due to local attraction of iron in the ship.

COMPASS VARIATION AND DEVIATION AND THEIR CORRECTIONS.

The earth is a vast natural magnet, but unfortunately the magnetic poles are not coincident with the earth's poles, nor is the magnetic equator coincident with the Equator; moreover, the magnetic poles are not fixed in position, but have a slow motion around the earth's surface.

The latest explanation of the directive force of the earth's magnetism on a compass needle regards the earth as an armature instead of a natural loadstone. The sun is constantly emitting streams of negatively-charged ions or corpuscles of electricity, and the earth is revolving on its axis from West to East in a negatively-charged electric field, cutting lines of force. Consequently, electric currents flowing North and South are generated on the earth's surface, just as currents are generated in the armature of a dynamo.

The North Magnetic Pole lies in about Lat. 70 degrees N., Long. 96 degrees W., and as the compass needle points to magnetic North, it is displaced to the left or right of true North, accordingly as our position is to the eastward or westward of the circle passing through the magnetic poles.

This angular displacement of the compass needle from true North is called the variation, and is noted on all charts. The variation is nearly constant at any given place, and the annual change, due to the slow motion of the magnetic poles, is given on the charts.

On our coast charts the compass rose is placed with the North-South line in the magnetic meridian, and if the navigator refers his courses and bearings to the nearest compass rose, variation need not trouble him. On general ocean charts, however, the compass roses are true; that is, the North-South line is true North, and dotted curves are drawn on the chart giving the variation for each change of a degree. Consequently, the navigator must apply the variation found on the chart to his magnetic course to find his true course to lay off on the chart.

When the compass needle is pulled to the right of true North, the variation is called Easterly, and marked plus; if the needle is pulled to the left of true North, the variation is Westerly and marked minus.

The lines of force of the earth's magnetism are only horizontal at the magnetic equator, and dip down as we near the magnetic poles, finally becoming vertical. As the compass needle is constrained to move in the horizontal plane, only the horizontal component of the earth's foce is of value in directing the needle, and at the magnetic poles a compass needle on shore will revolve freely.

DEVIATION.

The most important error to the navigator is that arising from the attraction of the iron on board ship, and differs on each ship. This is called deviation.

We know that if a piece of iron is brought near a magnet or compass it becomes temporarily magnetized and attracts the compass needle and will attract small pieces of iron. When removed from the vicinity of a magnet, this magnetism is soon lost. If, however, the iron or steel is twisted or subjected to blows while temporarily magnetized, the induced magnetism becomes more permanent, the length of time it will remain magnetic depending upon the quality of the metal, whether hard or soft. A steel bar can be magnetized by simply bringing it in the magnetic meridian and hammering it.

In the process of building, a ship lies on the stocks for a long while, with her head in the same direction, and every piece of iron or steel that enters into her making is subjected to violent hammering. Consequently a sub-permanent magnetism is induced in the hard metal parts. Immediately after launching, the ship is placed with her head in the opposite direction, so that the subsequent hammering may serve to neutralize this sub-permanent magnetism. A large portion of this magnetism does disappear, but sufficient remains to allow us, by an analysis of a ship's deviation table, to determine how she was heading while being built.

SELECTION OF COMPASS SITE.

Having an appreciation of the causes that produce compass errors, we can proceed to select the place for our compass. On account of the quadrantal deviation, we will locate our compass on the midship line, avoiding undue proximity to large masses of iron. On large ships one compass is always so located, known as the standard compass, and generally it is placed in an elevated position and giving as wide a view of the horizon as possible, so that compass bearings can be taken directly. Other compasses are placed near the steering wheel, and the course having been set by standard compass and the ship steadied upon it, the corresponding course is steered by the steering compass, being frequently checked by the deck officer. On yachts, however, the compass must be so placed as to be visible by the helmsman.

Having determined the site, the fore and aft line must be carefully determined, and if the compass is mounted on a binnacle stand, the stand is placed in position, adjusted until the lubber's point is in line with the keel, and the binnacle secured. If our compass is a portable one and placed on deck, the fore and aft line should be permanently marked, so that the compass lubber point can always be placed correctly. Having due regard to the helmsman, we should also place our compass so as to allow of bearings being taken directly.

PELORUS.

The Pelorus is a dumb (*i. e.*, having no magnet) compass card, fitted with sight vanes and mounted so that it can be set to any desired heading of the ship, and so placed as to give a view around the horizon. On large ships we find a Pelorus on the ends of the navigating bridge, and since it has no magnetic qualities, we may consult our convenience in placing it. Obviously, if we set the Pelorus to the same ship's heading as the standard compass, the line of sight through the sight vanes will give the compass bearing of any object.

We can accomplish the same object on yachts in a simple way. On top of the cabin, or some other convenient place, describe a circle, and mark where the fore and aft line crosses it. Now graduate your circle from the fore and aft marks, either to degrees or points, and, if you wish, mount a revolving arm with sight vanes. By sighting across this circle at any object, you can determine the number of points to the right or left of the fore and aft line it bears, and if we note the ship's head at that time a simple calculation gives the compass bearing of the object.

COMPASS DEVIATION.

With most of our sailing yachts built of wood compass deviations will probably be small and less than errors of steering or errors in reckoning leeway. But on motor boats, with engine aft and fuel tank forward, it may be difficult to find a compass site that is not close to disturbing masses of iron. Moreover, motor boats are always steered on a course, while sailing boats are often by the wind; so compass deviations, even when small, are of importance on motor boats. So having determined your

Ship's head by compass No.	Deviation	Ship's head by compass No.	Deviation	
NORTH	+ 30. 00	SOUTH	- 22. 30	W
N by E		S by W		
N NE	27. 30	S SW	- 13. 00	W
NE by N		SW by S		
NE	25. 00	SW	- 7. 00	W
NE by E		SW by W		
E NE	16. 30	W SW	- 5. 00	
E by N		W by S		
EAST	3. 45	WEST	- 5. 30	
E by S		W by N		
E SE	- 8. 30	W NW	- 6. 00	
SE by E		NW by W		
SE	- 18. 30 W	NW	- 3. 00	
SE by S		NW by N		
S SE	- 25. 30 W	N NW	+ 7. 00	
S by E		N by W		

A deviation card. Easterly deviation is marked plus; westerly, minus

deviations, if you cannot compensate your compass, make out a table giving the deviation on
each point, marking Easterly deviations plus,
Westerly deviations minus, and keep it handy
for reference—as in the compass box. Now if
you wish to steer North (magnetic) look at
your table. If you find the deviation for ship's
head North is one-quarter of a point Easterly,
your course by compass is North one-quarter
West. If your deviations are very large, say
two points Easterly, your course becomes
North-North-West, and the deviation on that
heading of the ship, which is probably different
from when heading North, should be used.

HOW TO DETERMINE DEVIATION.

There are four methods used for determining compass deviation—reciprocal bearings,
ranges, bearings of a distant object and bearings of the sun.

Reciprocal Bearings.—Send   a   compass
ashore, and set it up in some convenient place
free from local attraction. To test this set up
three marks about 20 feet from the compass in
a triangle. Set compass on each of these marks,
and observe the bearing of the other two marks.
The respective bearings of *A* from *B*, *B* from
A, should differ by 180 degrees, if there is no
local attraction.

Arrange with the observer on shore some

simple flag signal to indicate when observations are to be taken. Now swing ship by steaming in a circle, or if at anchor by springs and hawsers, or get a motor boat to tow you around. Steady ship on each heading (every other point is sufficient) for 4 minutes, signal shore observer, and take bearing of shore compass, the observer ashore at the signal taking the bearing of the ship's compass. His bearings reversed give his correct magnetic bearing from the ship, and the difference between this bearing and that given by the ship compass gives the compass deviation on each heading.

Ranges.—Take some definite range whose magnetic bearing you may take from the chart, and steam or sail across the range on different headings, giving your compass 4 minutes to steady, and as you cross the range observe its compass bearing and compare its bearing by the chart.

Bearings of a Distant Object.—If we have an object so distant that its bearing will not appreciably change while swinging ship, we can take its compass bearing on the required number of points as the ship swings around. Its magnetic bearing may be taken from the chart, or the average compass bearing on a number of equidistant points may be taken as the correct magnetic bearing (this assumes that your constant error is small).

Bearings of the Sun or Sun Azimuths.—On
large ships the azimuth circle is used with the
standard compass, but a simple method for observing the bearings of the sun with a compass
whose level is assured by being mounted in
freely swinging gimbals is as follows:

Set a long brass screw with flat head over
the center of the compass and observe the
bearing of its shadow—this bearing reversed is
the bearing of the sun. If you wish to use
your dumb compass marked on the cabin top,
take the shadow of a plumb line over the center.

When the sun is on the prime vertical, or
bears nearly East or West, its bearing changes
very slowly, and mistakes in time will not cause
great errors; consequently, if you are going to
use sun azimuths (or bearings), the observations should be taken early in the morning or
late in the afternoon.

Prepare beforehand your notebook by ruling
columns for ship's head, watch time, local apparent time, true bearing of the sun, observed
bearing, compass error, variation, deviation.
To find the local apparent time, assuming your
watch is set correctly to local standard time,
apply the difference in longitude between your
position and the standard meridian, adding it to
standard time if you are East of the standard
meridian, and *vice versa*. For instance, your
longitude is 76 degrees 15 minutes West, or 1

degree 15 minutes West of the 75th meridian.
This reduced to time is 5 minutes (there are 4
minutes to a degree, or an hour to 15 degrees),
and since you are West you must subtract 5
minutes from standard time, 75th meridian, to
get local mean time.

Our time is measured by the apparent motion
of the sun, but since this apparent motion is in
a plane called the Ecliptic, inclined to the
Equator, and, moreover, since the apparent
motion of the sun is not uniform in the plane,
being accelerated in the winter, retarded in the
summer, according as the earth is nearer or
farther from the sun, astronomers measure
time from a fictitious sun whose motion is uniform, called the mean or average sun. In the
Nautical Almanac (also Tide Tables), Table 6,
the difference of time between the apparent sun
and mean sun is given for each day of the year,
and is called the equation of time. So look in
the Nautical Almanac for the equation of time
and apply it to our local mean time, adding or
subtracting as indicated in the almanac, and we
have local apparent time.

Now swing ship, steadying on as many points
as desired, and observe the bearing of the sun,
noting the watch time.

Correct the watch time, writing down the
local apparent time for each observation. Referring now to the Azimuth Tables we find for

each day of the year opposite the local apparent time the true bearing of the sun is given. Enter these opposite your local apparent times.

The difference between the observed and the true bearing of the sun gives us our total compass error for each heading of the ship, so put these down in the compass error column, marking the error plus if the true bearing is to the right of the compass bearing, minus if to the left. This column is the deviation plus the local variation, so subtract the variation, marking Easterly variation plus, Westerly variation minus, and the result is the compass deviation on the ship's headings on which the observations were taken. Having our deviations on every other point, or nearly so, we can construct a curve that will give the deviations on the other points, and this will also show any material error in one of the observations.

Make out a table giving the compass deviations on each point, and keep it handy, so as to be able to apply the difference immediately to any course we may wish to steer.

If you are fortunate enough to possess a compass with a compensating binnacle, you can proceed to have it compensated, reducing the deviations to a maximum of 2 degrees.

TAKING BEARINGS FOR POSITION.

THE VALUE OF TAKING BEARINGS ON FIXED
OBJECTS TO DETERMINE THE EXACT POSI-
TION OF THE VESSEL. SOME SIMPLE FORMU-
LÆ THAT WILL BE OF GREAT HELP IN
NAVIGATING.

BY C. S. STANWORTH,
Commander U. S. Navy, Retired.

THE importance of keeping track of the
position of a vessel by frequent plotting
of cross-bearings on a chart cannot be
overestimated by the person entrusted with the
navigation. These positions carefully plotted
show any set of current or leeway, and when
taken frequently should give ample warning
when the course should be changed to avoid
shoals.

In the navy, when navigation marks are in
sight, the navigator is constantly assuring himself of the position of his ship by cross-bearings,
two bearings of the same object, single bearing,
sounding, etc., all of which he records in his
notebook, and then plots on the chart. If his
vessel runs ashore, the Court of Inquiry will call

for the chart on which the course of the vessel was plotted, and the navigator's notebook, and if these show that he has not taken advantage of every opportunity to verify his position, it will be more detrimental than an error in plotting. However, if bearings are taken frequently, an error in plotting or observing will probably be detected, as the position will not plot where expected. But, if you have not taken any bearings for some time, you do not know where they should plot, and hence you have no check.

The questions asked by the Board will be, "What navigation marks were in sight when the vessel grounded? How frequently were bearings taken? When was the last position determined and how?"

By navigation marks is meant not only lighthouses, buoys, etc., but any objects on the chart that can be identified, such as towers, points of land, islands, and above all, the marks on the leadline.

While yachtsmen are not subject to court-martial for running a vessel ashore, yet, if one is navigating a friend's yacht, the obligation is strong to give faithful, intelligent service. If, as owner, you are navigating your own vessel, besides the pleasure of knowing you are doing the work intelligently and well you should see that you are assuring the safety of your property. The question of insurance also comes in, for if a vessel is stranded on a well-charted coast in clear weather, the insurance company will very properly demand an inquiry into the methods of navigation in use, and neglect on the part of the navigator to take bearings may vitiate the insurance.

In navigating a boat in home waters, one soon becomes familiar with them, and by the relative position of objects and their apparent distance he *senses* his position. He has seen a lighthouse, say, in clear and hazy weather, and he instinctively allows for the condition of the atmosphere in judging his distance. He knows the set and drift of the currents, or his eye soon tells him. He is *piloting* his vessel, and does not need bearings.

He may have adventured once or twice outside of home waters, but he is unfamiliar with the size and appearance of lighthouses and the topography of the shore, and he feels a timidity that is only allayed when his course leads him close to a buoy that he can locate on the chart by its number.

To acquire the necessary confidence in your ability to guide a vessel over strange waters by a chart, let us assume that you know the errors of your compass on the different headings, and how to apply them to get the correct bearing of any object. Now, with the chart of your *home waters,* begin navigating by taking bearings, plotting them on the chart, laying off a compass course from that plotted position, and then steering that compass course, trying not to use your pilot knowledge unless necessary. When near a buoy or other charted object, take bearings, plot them, and see how close they will plot to your known position. If they do not plot close, it must be due to an error in observing or plotting, which you can remedy by more care. Or it may be due to using a wrong compass error. Take off from the chart the bearing of one of your objects, and compare the chart bearing with the observed bearing; the difference is the compass error for that heading. If you have used magnetic bearings, the difference is the deviation; if you have used true bearings, it is deviation plus variation.

When you find that your bearings are giving you good positions, then practice your pilot's eye. Having taken your bearings, mark on the chart where you think you are, then plot your position and compare the guess with the observed position. The object in this is to acquire the habit of piloting by chart, for in rainy or rough weather it may be inconvenient to plot your bearings, or in crooked channel work you may not have time. Keep a record of your bearings, however, and when occasion offers get a plotted position for verification. Having given yourself this training, you have learned to navigate or pilot by the chart, independent of local knowledge, and the only equipment necessary to enable you to extend your cruises are the charts.

HOW BEARINGS ARE TAKEN.

On large ships, the standard compass fitted with an azimuth circle is generally placed in an elevated position to remove it as far as possible from the iron of the ship, and this gives a view of the horizon. Bearings are taken directly with the azimuth circle by bringing the sight vanes in line with the object, and reading off the standard compass bearing, this bearing then being corrected for the deviation on that particular heading of the ship, giving the magnetic bearing.

In addition, provision is made for mounting a Pelorus at either end of the bridge, the Pelorus being a dumb compass card that can be clamped for any heading of the ship, and fitted with sight vanes. In using the Pelorus, the compass card is clamped at the same heading of the ship as that shown by the standard compass, and hence the bearings taken by the sight vanes on the Pelorus are the same as if taken with the standard compass.

On yachts the compass is often placed with

Table for finding the distance of an object by two bearings, and the distance run between them.

POINTS.	DIFFERENCE BETWEEN THE COURSE AND THE FIRST BEARING—POINTS.																	
Difference between the course and the SECOND bearing.	2	2½	3	3½	4	4½	5	5½	6	6½	7	7½	8	8½	9	9½	10	10½
4	1.00																	
4½	0.81	1.23																
5	0.69	1.00	1.45															
5½	0.60	0.85	1.17	1.66														
6	0.54	0.74	1.00	1.35	1.85													
6½	0.49	0.67	0.88	1.14	1.50	2.02												
7	0.46	0.61	0.79	1.00	1.27	1.64	2.17											
7½	0.43	0.57	0.72	0.90	1.11	1.39	1.77	2.30										
8	0.41	0.53	0.67	0.82	1.00	1.22	1.50	1.87	2.41									
8½	0.40	0.51	0.63	0.76	0.92	1.09	1.31	1.58	1.96	2.50								
9	0.39	0.49	0.60	0.72	0.85	1.00	1.18	1.39	1.66	2.03	2.56							
9½	0.38	0.48	0.58	0.69	0.80	0.93	1.08	1.25	1.46	1.72	2.08	2.60						
10	0.38	0.47	0.57	0.66	0.76	0.88	1.00	1.14	1.31	1.51	1.76	2.11	2.61					
10½	0.38	0.47	0.56	0.65	0.74	0.84	0.94	1.06	1.19	1.35	1.55	1.79	2.12	2.60				
11	0.39	0.47	0.56	0.64	0.72	0.81	0.90	1.00	1.11	1.24	1.39	1.57	1.80	2.11	2.56			
11½	0.40	0.48	0.56	0.63	0.71	0.79	0.87	0.95	1.05	1.15	1.27	1.41	1.58	1.79	2.08	2.50		
12	0.41	0.49	0.57	0.64	0.71	0.78	0.85	0.92	1.00	1.08	1.18	1.29	1.41	1.57	1.76	2.03	2.41	
12½	0.43	0.51	0.58	0.65	0.71	0.77	0.83	0.90	0.97	1.03	1.11	1.20	1.29	1.41	1.55	1.72	1.96	2.30

Note.—Table 5A in the American Practical Navigator (H. O. Publication No. 9) gives the same to quarter points.

Rule.—Multiply the distance run in the interval between the two bearings by the number found in the table under the difference between the course and first bearing, and opposite the difference between the course and the second bearing. The product is the distance at the time the second bearing was taken.

Example.—A lighthouse, when first seen, bore WNW.; after running W. by S. 16 miles, it bore N. ½ W. Required, its distance when the second bearing was taken.

Difference between course and first bearing. = 3 points.
Difference between course and second bearing.. = 8½ points.
Corresponding tabular number.............. = 0.63.
And 16 miles × 0.63 = 10.08 miles, the distance required.

no reference to the iron of the ship or with a view of the horizon. I was once asked to look at a compass on a new 75-foot yacht, as it was giving trouble. It was mounted on a low platform about two feet forward of the steering wheel, along the drum of which a steel tiller rope was continually shifting with the wheel, and while there was the usual amount of brass work aft, the compass platform had a galvanized iron railing and stanchions. On account of the tiller rope, you could not give a table of deviations. By substituting a bronze tiller rope and brass railing, the compass could have been made serviceable, but it was poorly placed for observing bearings.

When the compass is well situated for taking bearings, it should be fitted with an azimuth circle or sight vanes and bearings taken directly, thus avoiding any error in transposing bearings. If necessary to change course slightly to bring into view any object, change your course, allow the compass a couple of minutes to settle, take your bearings, and go back to the original course. You can now plot your bearings, using of course the compass error for the heading the ship was on when the bearings were taken.

If the compass is poorly placed, draw a circle on top of your cabin, mark off the fore and aft line, and divide the starboard and port semi-circles into 16 parts each, and mark the 32 points of the circle with short and long lines as a compass card is marked. Put a bushing in the center of the circle, and fit a wooden or metal arm with vertical pins at the ends to revolve in this bushing. You now have a dumb compass with sight vane. Take your bearings, recording them as so many points on starboard bow or quarter, port bow or quarter; also take the heading by compass. A simple calculation will give the compass bearing of the object.

For instance, Horton's Point bore 7 points on starboard bow, and Cornfield Lightvessel bore 3 points on port bow, course E. by S. Then, Horton's Point bore S., Cornfield bore E.N.E.

Bearings can be taken with some accuracy by lining your hand across the compass, and it is an excellent practice to obtain the approximate bearing in this way before using your dumb compass, for you not only test the accuracy of lining up, but you avoid any serious error in transposing your dumb compass bearing, since you know about what it should be.

CROSS-BEARINGS OF TWO OBJECTS.

The simplest method of establishing the position of a vessel on a chart is to observe the compass bearing of two charted objects, correct these compass bearings by applying the total compass error for that heading of the ship, and

with the aid of a protractor and the nearest
meridian line, draw lines through the observed
objects at the angles of the true bearings.   Or
you may use the parallel rulers and the nearest
compass rose, being careful to use the *true* compass rose if you have corrected the compass
bearings for deviation and variation, the *magnetic* compass rose if you have corrected only
for deviation.   The intersection of these two
lines on the chart will give you the position, and
the nearer the intersection is to a right angle
the better.

Since lighthouses are the principal navigation
marks, both by day and night, you can enhance
the value of your charts by having a rubber
stamp of a compass rose made, and imprinting
a compass rose with center at each lighthouse,
being careful to have the North-South line of
the compass rose coincident with the meridian
line of you wish to use true bearings, or with
magnetic N. if you wish to use magnetic bearings.   Now when you take a bearing of a lighthouse, after correcting it, lay your ruler along
the compass rose at the lighthouse, and you
have no shifting of ruler to do.

TWO BEARINGS OF THE SAME OBJECT.

Very often, especially along the coast, we
have only one object in sight which we can iden-

tify on the chart.   Now, if we take a bearing of
this object, observe carefully our course and distance run, and after changing the bearing 3 or
more points we again take it, we can determine
our position, for we have a triangle in which the
distance run is the base, and the angles at the
base are determined by the difference between
our course and the two lines of bearings.   We
can use the subjoined table, and with the data
there given, pick out the distance of the object
at the second bearing, which gives our position.

It will be more convenient and certainly more
gratifying to the eye, to work out this triangle
graphically on the chart with the aid of the
parallel rulers and compass rose.

Take your first bearing, correct it, and draw
it on the chart, marking your probable position
on it.   Through this position draw a line representing your course.   After running a certain
distance, the bearing has changed 3 or more
points.   Take the second bearing, correct it,
and draw on the chart, also mark off on your
course the distance run.   If the distance run
coincides with the intersection of the second line
of bearing and the line representing the course,
this is your position.   In all probability it will
not, so with your parallel rulers draw a line
through the point representing the distance run,
and parallel to the first bearing.   Where this
line intersects the second line of bearing will be

your position, provided your distance run represents the distance over the bottom, or in other words you have had no current, for I presume that you have the means, patent or chip log or engine revolutions, to determine your speed through the water.

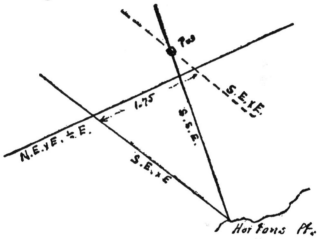

Fig. 1.—Finding distance by two bearings on same object

As an example suppose you are running to the eastward in Long Island Sound, hugging the south shore on account of flood tide and a strong easterly wind, and have sighted Horton's Point on your starboard bow when it shuts in thick. Your course is N.E. by E. ½ E., speed 7 knots, and presently you sight Horton's Point bearing S.E. by E. (magnetic), which you put on your chart, where you already have your course line

drawn. Fifteen minutes later, Horton's Point
bears S.S.E., and laying off 1.75 knots along
your course from the point of intersection of
the first line of bearing, you draw through this
a S.E. by E. line, and also through Horton's
Point a S.S.E. line (the second bearing).
Where these two lines intersect is your position.
(See Fig. 1.)

Or, having the following data: distance run
1.75 knots, course N.E. by E. ½ E., first bearing S.E. by E., second bearing S.S.E., you can
use the table, and at 5½ points vertical column,
8½ points horizontal column, we find the unit
distance 1.58, which multiplied by 1.75 sea
miles, our distance run, gives 2.7; or at time
of second bearing Horton's Point bore S.S.E.,
distance 2.7 sea miles. (See rules given with
table.)

IMPORTANCE OF SOUNDINGS.

It is an excellent practice to take a sounding
whenever you take bearings, for if you have
gotten good cross-bearings, the sounding gives
a check. In the case of bearings on a single
object, soundings should be taken at each bearing, for from it you may often determine
whether you have a current or not.

Suppose when Horton's Point bore S.E. by
E. you sounded and had 11 fathoms—you
would have a fairly good position at once. At

the second bearing you find 9 fathoms which agrees with the chart at the intersection of the lines of bearings. You will notice on your chart that if you continue on your course for 15 minutes you will pass over a 5-fathom bank; so if it shuts in thick again, you will by sounding be able to check your position. If your sounding when Horton's Point bore S.S.E. had been less than 9 fathoms, it would have shown you that you had allowed too much for distance run, or in other words had a current against you, and for your bearing to have shifted 3 points in less than 1.75 miles you must be closer to Horton's Point than 2.7 miles.

DOUBLING THE BOW ANGLE.

If we take our first bearing when the object is, say, 3 points on the bow, and wait until this angle is doubled, or the object is 6 points on the bow, the triangle formed by the two lines of bearing and the course line will be an isosceles triangle, and the distance run will be equal to the distance the object is at the second bearing. If the object was "on the bow," *i.e.*, four points or 45° off our course, the double angle will be 8 points or 90°, and the distance run will be the distance of the object when abeam. (See Fig. 2.) This "bow and beam" bearing should always be taken when passing lighthouses, and an entry made in log or notebook, "At ——

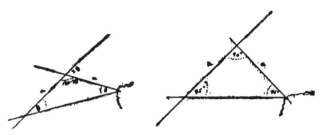

Fig. 2.—Diagram of bow and beam bearing. When bearing of an object is doubled, its distance will be equal to that run by the vessel between the two bearings.

passed —— Lighthouse bearing ——, distance —— miles, course ——."

On account of an off-lying shoal, you may wish to know beforehand at what distance your course will take you clear of a point of land or lighthouse. In this case, note your patent log when the object bears 26½ degrees on the bow, and again when it bears 4 points or 45 degrees on the bow. The distance run will be the distance off when the object is abeam; 26½ degrees is nearly 2¼ points. (See Fig. 3.) We construct the 45° triangle first, and lay off BA equal to BC equal to CL; then by construction, tangent of angle CAL is equal to $\frac{CL}{AC}$ or ½ or .5. Angle CAL is equal to 26° 34′.

POSITION BY BEARING OF THREE OBJECTS.

Obviously, if we know the error of our compass and apply it correctly, lines of bearings from any number of objects will intersect in the

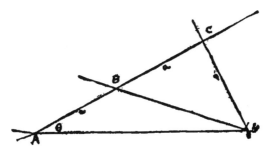

Fig. 3.—Diagram of 26½° and 45° bearings

same point (the change of position of the vessel while bearings are being taken being negligible). Consequently, when we establish our position by cross-bearings, if we take the bearing of a third object, we have a reliable check on our work. We will rarely find that the three bearings meet in a common point, but instead their intersection will form a triangle, the size of which will be directly proportional to the error of our work. However, we can by inspection of this triangle estimate closely our position.

Suppose we are at such a position in Long Island Sound that Horton's Point bears S.E. by S. ⅛ S. (or S.S.E. ⅞ E.), Falkner Island Light bears N.W., Westerly, Cornfield Light-vessel bears E.N.E. ⅝ E., Branford Reef Light bears N.W. by W. ⅜ W.

If we draw these lines on the chart we will find that they meet in a common point as

shown in the sketch (Fig. 4) by dot and dash
lines.

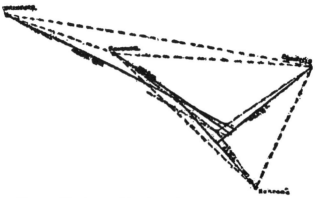

Fig. 4.—Plotting position for a four-point bearing with an
unknown compass error. Dot and dash lines, correct bearings; full lines, observed bearings.

Now, suppose our compass had an unknown
compass error of one-quarter point easterly
deviation on that heading.

This would make our bearings become Horton's Point, S.E. ⅞ S., Falkner Island,
N.W. ¼ W., Westerly, Cornfield, E.N.E. ⅜
E.; Branford, N.W. by W ⅝ W. which
lines are drawn in full on the sketch. Now
consider the triangle formed by the first three
lines, in which our true point lies inside of the
main triangle formed by connecting Horton's,
Falkner, and Cornfield. Here we find that our
true point lies *inside* the small triangle formed
by the intersection of the three lines of bearings.

If we consider Branford, Falkner and Corn-field, where our true point lies outside of the main triangle, we find it lies *outside* of the small triangle formed by the intersection of the three lines of bearing, and *what is important,* it is on the same side of the line of bearing from the most distant object (in this case Branford) as the intersection of the other two lines of bear-ings (from Falkner and Cornfield).

Knowing these two laws and having drawn our lines of bearings from three objects, we can estimate quite closely our true position. Or we can take a sheet of tracing paper and lay off from a common point, using a protrac-tor or the compass rose on the chart, our three lines of bearing, marking each line with the name of its object. Place the tracing paper on the chart and move it until the lines pass through their respective objects, then prick through the center, which is your position. From the chart take the bearing of this point and any of your observed objects, preferably the more distant. The difference between the bearing taken from the chart and the bearing you observed will give you your compass error.

RANGES.

If our vessel crosses the prolongation of a line joining any two charted objects, these objects are *seen* to come in line, or *on range*. This range is a fixed line of bearing and can be drawn on the chart beforehand. Now, if at the

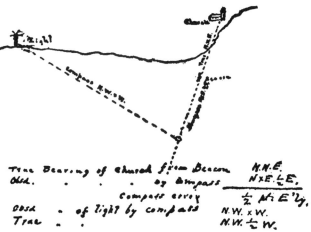

Fig. 5.—Taking a range bearing to correct compass error

moment of crossing the range a bearing of another object is taken, we have a very accurate position, for one line of bearing is exact, and errors can only affect the other line. Moreover, by taking our compass bearing of the more distant object in range and comparing it with the bearing on the range taken from the chart, we can at once determine our compass error and apply it to the second bearing. We take the bearing of the more distant object on range as it is changing less rapidly. Fig 5 shows this clearly.

KEEPING THE LOG.

BY CHARLES H. HALL.

ABOARD ship the history of each day's happenings, with the courses steered, speeds, notes of the weather, and all observations, is written in a volume called the Log Book. This record of events may be kept with great detail, as the navy regulations require, or may be reduced to a few brief notes. In deciding on the form in which the log is to be kept due regard must be paid to the conditions of use. A battleship's log book is written up with greater fullness than the record of a torpedo boat. So also the form suitable for a large steam yacht would not be a proper one for a small motor boat manned by an amateur crew.

For the average Corinthian to attempt a man-of-war log seems a tremendous undertaking, yet if done systematically an approximation to it will require astonishingly little effort. Nevertheless it would be needless labor to record all the minutiæ of the day's proceedings, with the wind, weather, etc., from hour to hour. But the more that is set down, the greater will be the pleasure in reading over the record of past cruises, and the simpler it will be to collect a claim from the underwriters in case of damage.

Whatever form is adopted should be kept regularly, as it is annoying, to say the least, to find the log of one watch entered in good shape and that of the next almost a blank. It should be remembered that entries must often be made at night and in wet weather, so the form adopted should not be too ambitious, lest there be frequent gaps in the record.

One thing to bear in mind is that the log is, or should be, an inviolable record; an entry once made must not be erased or altered, or the value of the entire history is lessened. If a mistake be made let the original entry stand and write the correction above it or in the margin with a line through or around the erroneous note. If reasonable care is taken with times, courses, bearings, etc., the mistakes should be very few and usually easily noticed and corrected.

There is a certain minimum that must be set down if the log book is to have any value for navigating. This comprises times, courses and speeds or distances. The time referred to is the time of any event, such as getting up anchor, letting go anchor, changing course, sighting a lighthouse or other landmark, stopping or slow-ing the engine, taking a bearing or making a sounding to fix position.

The course should be the course steered, with the magnetic course also. The speed must be the actual speed through the water, derived, in the case of a power boat, from engine revolutions compared with a carefully made Speed-Revolutions curve, or else from patent log, chip log, or a tested speed-indicator. The ordinary *guess* speed is worse than useless. There should also be a column for remarks. Such a log may be kept in a form like this:

Time	Course C. M.	Course P. C.	Speed	Remarks

It may be kept in a small note book (preferably with pencil attached), using the left-hand page for the first four columns and the right-hand page for the fifth. The book should be well made with good paper and a binding that will not disintegrate with the first few drops of water that strike it. It should be of decent size so that the entries need not be crowded. Remember that entries must frequently be made by the faint light of the binnacle lamp or the rays of a deck lantern. Sometimes the book must be held under the skirts of an oilskin coat while brief notes of bearings are hurriedly jotted down.

The above example may be considered merely the dry bones of log. A more ambitious form is given below, though some of the columns will doubtless be found blank after a rainy, blowy night. Still, so many entries may be made with symbols that a little effort will keep the record well filled.

Such a log approaches the standard of a naval vessel or large deep water ship, and contains the necessary data for the navigator. Those who have turned out for the middle watch on a black night will appreciate the value of such a history of the previous watch. How often the man relieved has simply pointed out a light or two, giving no idea of distance or bearings taken, yawned, and gone below for a "caulk." For all the information transmitted the boat might be miles out of her proper position and making but a fraction of the usual speed. But where the log has been kept in good style the new "officer of the deck" can check up the position and speed, get some idea as to weather probabilities, predict the time of sighting lighthouses and the bearing on which to look for them, and, in general, navigate with confidence.

The form illustrated above contains a number of columns. The first, headed Time, refers as before to the time of any event. If these events (anchoring, changing course, etc.) are

Time	Course C.M.	Course P.C.	Speed	R.P.M.	Pat Log	WIND Direction	WIND Force	Sea	Weather	Clouds	Bar.	REMARKS

Form of log used on a large ship

regularly entered in the Remarks column the Time column will contain only the hours at which the weather observations are made. When different men take charge successively the same watch or clock should be used for navigating, or all their watches set to the same standard.

"Course C. M." is the *correct magnetic* course as obtained from the chart, with variation alone allowed for. "Course P. C." means course *per compass* and refers to the course actually steered after making corrections for deviation, tidal current, leeway, etc.

While anchored, the course columns should have the entry "At anchor" and the direction of the boat's head may be noted so that one can tell when she swings. In crooked channels some general note such as "Standing down East channel," or "Entering Harbor," may be made as the vessel is being *piloted*, not *navigated*.

The fourth column, Speed, should have the speed in knots; don't confuse this with the speed in statute miles, but get the habit of using nautical miles for distances and knots for speeds for all navigational work.

Column five, R. P. M., need not be completely filled, as the engine revolutions should not vary greatly unless weather and sea conditions change. Taking the engine revolutions once or twice during a watch should ordinarily give sufficient data.

The entries in the sixth column are important; and the patent log (if used) should be read and noted every hour and at each change of course, on passing every light, at the time of each sounding (for fixing position), when taking bearings, etc. If the patent log is correct, or if its error be known and applied, an unsuspected or improperly estimated current will be discovered in good season.

There are two spaces headed Wind; one, Direction, the other, Force. The direction of the *true* wind is to be logged, not that of *apparent* wind. As a boat moves, the direction of the apparent wind is always further forward than the true wind. The direction of the latter should always be known and may be obtained by noting the surface ripples, flags on boats at anchor, manœuvres of sailing craft, and other indications. It is especially important to have this knowledge at night. By day one sees a sailing vessel a long distance away and can tell her course. At night nothing but a side-light or "flare-up" is seen and the course must be inferred from the direction of the *true* wind.

The force of the wind is measured on Beaufort's Scale, a notation giving to different velocities of wind different values on an arbitrary scale ranging from zero to twelve. Yachtsmen will seldom have to log any wind over force 9 on this scale. A wind of force 5 is a reefing breeze for fair-sized racing craft, in fact many careful skippers will turn in a reef when the wind gets above fifteen miles an hour.

Here is Beaufort's Scale. "Sail carried" refers to deep-water ships with old-time single topsails:

BEAUFORT'S SCALE

HOURLY VELOCITY IN MILES.	SCALE	STATE.	SAIL CARRIED.
	0	Calm	
1	1	Light airs......	Steerage way
2 to 3	2	Light breeze....	Clean full, 1 to 2 knots
4 to 7	3	Gentle breeze....	Clean full, 3 to 4 knots
9 to 15	4	Moderate breeze	Clean full, 5 to 6 knots
15 to 18	5	Fresh breeze....	With royals
19 to 22	6	Strong breeze...	Topgallant sails over single reefs
23 to 28	7	Moderate gale..	Two reefs in topsails
28 to 40	8	Fresh gale......	Three reefs in topsails
40 to 48	9	Strong gale.....	Close-reefed topsails and courses
48 to 56	10	Whole gale.....	Close-reefed topsails and reefed foresail
57 to 80	11	Storm	Storm staysails
80 to 100	12	Hurricane	Bare poles

(From Qualtrough's Sailor's Handy Book)

When the big ships start to reef topsails it's time for small fry to think about a snug anchorage, and when it gets up to a whole gale "it's no place for a gentleman's son!"

The column headed Sea refers to the state of the sea, as smooth, rough, moderate, choppy, tide rips and so on. The entries are made with initials only as S, R, M, C, T, etc. The Weather column is also filled with symbols, of which there is quite a system. Most of these are initials, though there are some exceptions; thus *q* means squally and *h* stands for hail and not haze.

WEATHER SYMBOLS

(From Qualtrough)

b	Represents	Blue sky
c	"	Clouds (detached)
d	"	Drizzling rain
f	"	Foggy
g	"	Gloomy
h	"	Hail
l	"	Lightning
m	"	Misty (hazy)
p	"	Passing showers
q	"	Squally
r	"	Rain
s	"	Snow
t	"	Thunder
u	"	Ugly (threatening)
v	"	Visibility (objects at a distance very distinct)
w	"	Wet (dew)

"A bar under any letter augments its signification; thus *f*, very foggy; *r*, heavy rains, etc."

So we see that several symbols may be set down together, and they (with the entries in other columns) will give a pretty fair idea of the weather. For instance, r. h. t. l. means rain, hail, thunder and lightning; b. c. indicates blue sky and detached clouds; g. p., gloomy with passing showers. When we find u. q. in the weather column, with an easterly wind of increasing strength (say force 6 or 7) and a steadily falling barometer, we may infer that "the walking is bad."

The Clouds column is for the proportion of clouds to blue sky; one system gives o as a clear sky and 10 as a sky entirely covered. The practice in the navy is just the opposite, the heading being "Proportion of blue sky, in tenths," 10 indicating a clear sky and o one completely overcast.

The "Bar." column is for the readings of the barometer. These should be set down in inches and hundredths, 30.28, 29.43, and so on. The ordinary aneroid has only the even hundredths marked so that the odd ones must be estimated. The entries in the last six columns mentioned (from Direction of Wind to Bar.) should be made regulary, preferably on the hour, but at least every two hours. They need not be made at the odd intervals of time, as when taking bearings, etc.

This brings us to the heading Remarks, under which the history of all the day's doings is recorded. Aside from the navigational notes, anything of interest should be set down, such as taking aboard gasolene, oil stores or water, with the quantity of each and the price paid; members of the ship's company leaving or joining; any unusual happening in the harbor, and so on. These notes should be made *at the time,* and not written up a day or two later. As the space is generally restricted such entries are necessarily condensed; indeed, "log book brevity" is proverbial. The log book records of important naval engagements are startlingly short.

The navigational notes must always be written down at once and exactly as they were taken. No "doctoring" is allowable. If a set of bearings does not plot properly, try again and you will probably find the error. Always enter the remarks systematically. The habit is worth cultivating, and can be easily acquired. The following examples may be suggestive.

Here's one for taking the departure: "10.23 A. M., Execution Lt. bearing NW¼N dist. ¼m., changed course to ENE½E C.M., set pat. log reading 17.4." In this case the previous entries under Course have been "Proceeding up East River." The bearing and distance of the lighthouse give the position exactly. The reading of the patent log when first put overboard must be recorded.

For a cross bearing: "11.55 P. M., Gt. Capt. Id. Lt. NNW½W p.c., Green's Lodge Lt.

NE½N p.c., Eaton's Pt. Lt. ESE p.c., Ship's head ENE p.c., Pat. log. 30.0." These bearings are plotted on the chart immediately and fix the vessel's position.

The patent log reading gives the distance run through the water and serves as a check on the speed. It also shows whether the effect of the tidal current has been correctly estimated.

For passing a light: "2.15 P. M. Stratford Shoal Lt. abeam, dist. ¼ m. est., bearing N¼W, Pat. log. 48.7." This checks the correctness of the course laid and gives a new departure if the vessel is not in the position expected. ("Est." means estimated.)

For a change of course: "6.27 P. M. Cornfield Pt. L. V. abeam, dist. ½ m. Pat. log. 83.1, changed course to E⅛S C. M." This gives the position, a check on speed and tidal current, and a new departure for the next leg of the run.

When sighting an important landmark: "1.33 A. M. sighted Gay Head Lt. bearing E x S p.c., Vin. Sd. L. V. E x N p.c., Ship's head E½N p.c., Pat. log. 143.1."

The abbreviations used above are simple, Vin. Sd. L. V. means Vineyard Sound Light Vessel. When this data is plotted it shows whether the light is found on the expected bearing or not; if not, there has been an error in correcting the course for deviation, leeway, or current, and a new course must be worked out and set. The bearing of the lightship helps to fix the position. Estimating distance from a light (especially at night) is always exceedingly difficult, and cross bearings should be taken whenever an opportunity presents itself.

When anchoring: "7.50 A. M. Anchored off Nantucket Harbor Entrance in 4 fm. Port anchor, 15 fm. cable. Brandt Pt. Lt. NNW ½ W p.c., Great Pt. Lt. NE ½ E p.c., Ship's head ESE p.c." Here again cross bearings fix the position and show if the boat drags her anchor, though for this latter purpose cross ranges are far better. Cross ranges will also be useful in trying to locate an anchor that has been lost. They may be set down somewhat as follows: "Brown church spire in range with brick factory chimney, ENE. Outer spindle just open to N'd of town dock."

When sounding for locating your position: "8.17 P. M., Pat. log. 47.4, 12 fm. sand; 8.27 P. M. Pat. log. 48.8, 10 fm. white sand black specks; 8.40 P. M. Pat. log. 50.1, 8 fm. mud."

Keeping such a record as the above may prove too laborious for the average man, but will be very helpful to the navigator if properly filled out and will add to the pleasure of the winter's "fireside cruises."

But the entries made in any log must be written down as soon as possible after the events they describe have occurred. If a light

is passed, make a note of it *at once;* the same
with a bearing.   Half an hour later the recol-
lection will not be absolutely clear and a bearing may be improperly written or the time set
down wrongly.   So form the habit of recording
things as they happen.   Above all, *no faking!*
Better a blank page or the bare note of leaving
one port and arriving at another than a circum-
stantial account worked up a day or two late.
Sometimes there is very little to write in the
Remarks column, especially after a quiet watch
at anchor, but as our captain told us in '98:
"You can always generalize about the weather
when there's nothing else to write."

Those who desire more than the first form
given and yet do not wish to undertake such an
extensive record as the second one, may take a
middle course between them, retaining the most
essential columns for the particular kind of
cruising being done.

Regular printed log books may be bought
from dealers in nautical supplies but they are
generally designed for sea-going craft or large
yachts and have some spaces that will never be
filled on the average small packet.   They are
also apt to be rather bulky to stow away on a
boat where every inch is precious.   With the
home-make book the navigator may have as
many or as few columns as suits his fancy, the
book can be small to tuck away in the binnoc-

ular rack or similar receptacle, or even in the pocket.

The binnacle seems to offer an inviting stowage place—but *don't!* Never stow anything in the binnacle or near the compass; some day a bit of steel or iron may get there and cause no end of trouble.

On sailing craft, whenever sail is set, reefed or furled it should be noted, also every time she tacks, except, of course, when working along the beach with a series of short boards off and on.

Inaccuracy in the time gives one a wrong estimate of the speed. How often one sees the skipper work out of the harbor, and, when well outside, look at his watch and guess at the time elapsed since leaving. When entering the next port no one thinks of noting the time of passing some charted mark but, after everything is snugged down, some one pulls out his watch and guesses at the time of anchoring. Then with this time from port to port and the distance run (often overestimated) an hourly speed is figured out (neglecting all fractions or working them toward the fast side) that may be half a knot or more in excess of the true speed.

An important race comes along and the owner borrows a navigator whose first question is, "What can she make?" If he figures on the speed given him he will do some thinking while waiting for lights to be sighted or making the landfall after a run with the tidal current at an angle with the course.   Carelessness about time and distance is responsible for most of the "talk speeds" of yachts, and of many commercial boats, too.   A certain famous commodore of the New York Yacht Club used to say that his flagship could make eleven knots—and lick any sixteen-knot packet in the fleet!

PICKING UP THE MAN OVERBOARD

HOW TO ACT IN EMERGENCIES ON EITHER SAIL
OR POWER BOATS.

BY CHARLES H. HALL.

W HEN anything out of the way occurs on a sail boat it is the seaman's natural instinct to put the helm down. In the majority of cases this action is the proper one, as in the event of parting any gear the strain upon rigging and spars is usually reduced by bringing the boat up into the wind. But it must be remembered that there are exceptions, and that it may be better at times to put the helm up instead of down.

When any one falls overboard the essential thing is to get him out of the water as soon as possible, and, with the average small yacht, it will almost always be quicker to pick him up with the yacht herself than with the dinghy. So the sooner she can be brought back to the unfortunate one the better, especially as there is always the chance that he may have been injured by the fall or dazed by the shock of his sudden immersion.

Of course the very first thing to do is to throw over a life buoy of some sort, landing it *between the swimmer and the boat,* as one generally turns toward the boat in an effort to regain her before she sweeps past. So there should always be a life ring within reach of the helmsman, and it should not be "stopped" to anything nor toggled in any way, but must be held so that it may be released *instantly.* As good a way as any is to have the life ring held by a couple of straps, one across it a little below the center and the other running from this one down under the bottom of the ring. In an emergency there is no time to cast off stops or fiddle with a toggle, especially as excitement is apt to make thumbs of fingers ordinarily deft. If canvas seems too plain for these straps, they may be made of polished brass or copper, and will then be very neat in appearance, though no more serviceable.

Sometimes one sees a lanyard on the life buoy, but this is a mistake, as the ring will be torn from the grasp, or the person towed under if he manages to cling fast. Those who have tried being towed by a rope's end will realize this. Make it a habit to have the life ring in its place all the time, as one can never tell when it will be needed, and it will probably be wanted very badly if at all.

It is well to practice picking up objects

thrown overboard under different conditions of
sea and weather, taking the time with a stop
watch, so that a comparison of the different
methods may be made. Keep one eye on the
man in the water, as it is surprising how quickly
things go astern, and how confusingly they
change their bearings when the boat is manœuvering. In the navy there are men detailed
to keep their eyes on the man to be rescued,
and report or signal his direction. On a yacht
there are seldom enough hands to permit this,
but a sharp watch should be kept on the
unfortunate swimmer.

With a sailing craft on the wind many advo-
cate coming about at once. If this is done the
yacht is bound to gain a certain amount of
room to windward, and must then run down
to the man and round to. There is always the
chance of getting in irons, which would be
fatal, and the going about takes time. Then
the yacht has too much way on to pick the man
up on the run to leeward and must go past him
and round to again to get him. The quickest
method will be to jibe her around at once. This
will bring her down to leeward of him in a
very short space of time. Then, too, she will
be heading for him and may be "shaken along"
right up to the man without having too much
headway. This method keeps the boat under
control all the time and is far quicker than

making a tack, a run, and a round to. Of
course, it means lively work with backstays and
runners, and there may be occasions when the
wind is too strong to permit jibing with safety,
but sheets need not be started until the last
minute. It is surprising to see what a strong
wind one can jibe in on a pinch.

When reaching, this method will be found
still more rapid, for the main sheet will have to
be got aft to tack with certainty, while one can
jam the helm up and make a "North River
jibe" in an emergency such as this if the breeze
is not too strong, and only room to manœuver
in properly will be gained to leeward. Of
course such a jibe, without trimming in the
main sheet, will put quite a strain on spars and
gear, and must not be attempted if the wind is
fresh.

With the wind on the quarter or astern,
especially if blowing at all strong, coming about
will be the best scheme. In this case sheets
must be tended whichever way she comes
around, and better control may be had by tacking. Care must be taken to keep her going
while getting the main sheet aft, so that she
may have good headway for staying, and not
leave any possibility of getting in irons. Even
when working as fast as one can, a considerable
distance will be made to leeward before the
boat can be brought around. She can then be

sailed up to the man, heading for a point a little to leeward of him so as to allow for rounding to and shaking her along, thus having her headway checked when alongside. It is hard enough to pick up a small object, such as a cap, when the boat is moving rapidly through the water; it is almost impossible to lift out a heavy body, such as a man, when she has much way on. Then, too, the man may be exhausted by his efforts or stunned by a blow on the head from the jib sheet blocks or the boom, and unable to help himself.

So much for the "windjammers." With a motor boat the problem is a great deal simpler, as the direction of the wind need not be considered at all unless it is blowing hard. The thing to do is to get back to the man just as quickly as one can, and it makes little difference which way the helm is put. At first sight it might be thought that stopping and backing would be the thing, but this will generally take longer than turning around. Besides, few boats handle at all well when going astern and there is always the danger of the sharp edges of the propeller cutting the luckless man. The first thing to do is to throw out the clutch for a few seconds, to stop the motion of the propeller until the man is astern of it and thus lessen chances of his injuring himself on its knife-like blades, at the same time putting the helm hard over. This will give her a sheer in the desired direction, as she will not appreciably lose headway.   Then let the clutch in again and swing her around all the way, meeting her with the helm in time to straighten her up nicely and slow down as you get near the man.   Then back hard to check her way, taking care not to have the screw moving when the swimmer is near it.

It is not a matter of indifference which way the turn is made, as all single screw vessels turn more to one side than the other.   A boat with a right-hand propeller will usually be found to turn a little more easily to starboard than to port.   But the difference is slight and often not noticeable.   Experiments with the boat in smooth water will show if any difference exists. It may be found that she will turn more easily to one side at low speed and to the opposite side at high speed.   Of course in an emergency the turn must be made whichever way she will go the quickest, unless there is some obstruction on that side.

In a power boat it is just as important to have the life ring always at hand and ready for instant use as in a sailing craft.   And it must be dropped between the man and the boat, as a man naturally turns toward the boat as he comes to the surface, no matter what sort of packet he falls from.   The great thing, however, is to keep cool and set about the work of rescue methodically. If one has practiced picking up a life ring, deck bucket, or some similar object, the act of getting a man out of the water will be comparatively easy. If no practice has been had there is a good chance for some one to become confused and do the wrong thing, such as hitting the luckless man with the life buoy in the effort to land it close to him, putting the helm the wrong way, coming up with too much headway on, or some similar error. Whoever sees any one fall over the side must give the alarm at once and not be afraid to yell it out; at times such as this seconds count.

The habit of being prepared for an accident is a valuable one to acquire. When in charge of a boat plan what you would do if certain things should happen; then if an emergency arises you will be prepared for it and will probably do the right thing almost without thinking. Rear-Admiral Luce has this to say about emergencies:

"The habit cannot be too earnestly recommended to the young officer of anticipating various emergencies and casualties, such as a man falling overboard, parting rigging, etc., etc., and determining what should be done in each event, that when it does occur, the right order may burst involuntarily from the lips, and the mind be fully prepared for the necessary evolution. The habit may be cultivated while young, and will be found of the utmost advantage. An officer, while in charge of the deck, should never allow his thoughts to wander from the subject of his immediate duties, to which end it would be well, during his earlier years, to adopt as an invariable rule the resolution never to think of anything but *seamanship* while actually on watch." Further, he says: "You are suddenly startled by the cry of 'A man overboard.' There is nothing on board of a vessel that creates for the moment a greater excitement, or spreads a more general panic over the whole crew. Their best feelings and energies are suddenly excited, and forgetful of every other consideration than that of extending an arm to save a fellow-being, they rush aft in a body, without a thought or settled purpose of action. Here the influence of the officer must be exerted promptly and on the instant to turn their feelings and energies in the proper direction to the only mode of rescue. . . . A little exercise in picking up buoys, under various circumstances at sea, will rob the 'startling cry' of much of its terror, and accustom both the officer of the deck and the watch to that kind of work."

As to keeping the life-saving gear always in working order, the Admiral remarks: "Nearly every one of any experience at sea has some favorite little reminiscence to narrate of loss of

life by drowning, nor do they fail to relate, in
many cases, how the 'poor fellow' *might* have
been saved 'but for a marine's shirt stopped
to the boat's fall,' or something equally for-
tuitous.''

In Knight's "Modern Seamanship" we find:
"The most immediate danger to a man falling
overboard from a steamer is that of being
struck by the propeller. This danger is especially great in the case of a vessel with twin
screws, and is, of course, increased in any case
by throwing the stern to the side on which the
man has gone over. . . . The first thought of
a man falling overboard should be to swim
outward from the ship, and the first thought of
the officer on the bridge should be to stop, *not
back,* the engines. If it is known from which
side the man has fallen, the helm may be put
hard over to the opposite side, thus throwing
the stern away from him. This calls for quick
thinking and prompt action. . . . One or more
life buoys should be thrown at once. If a little
presence of mind is exercised here, it is often
possible to throw one of these very close to the
man. . . . Observations upon the turning
circles of a large number of steamers show that
a steamer turning with hard-over helm will pass
within a short distance—rarely so much as a
ship's length—from the point where the helm
was put down. No doubt the symmetry of the

curve may be considerably modified by wind
and sea, but not sufficiently to prevent a return
to the neighborhood of the starting point. The
time required for the full turn will vary with
the length of the ship, the speed, the weather
and the manœuvering powers of the vessel.
Every officer should know the manœuvering
powers of his own vessel, especially the size of
the turning circle, the time required to describe
it, and how close the ship will come to a marker
thrown over just before putting down the helm.
It will, of course, be understood that in turning,
speed must be regulated according to the conditions of the weather. It would not do, for
example, to come up into a heavy sea at full
speed."

The Navy "Boat Book" says, speaking of
the duties of the men at the life buoys: "They
must, therefore, know *how* to let go the life
buoy, and *when* to let it go. . . . The question
as to *when* to let the life buoy go requires in-
telligence and composure. A cool, intelligent
lookout will let the buoy drop within a few
feet of the man overboard, while if somewhat
excited or if he does not clearly understand his
duties, he may drop it long before the man is
abreast the buoy, or long after he has passed.
At the call 'Man overboard,' the life-buoy
lookout should endeavor instantly to ascertain
the side on which the man fell and to *get sight*

of him. Then drop the buoy as soon as possible *after* the man is abreast the buoy, so that it will be between him and the ship, toward which he naturally faces and swims. . . . Signalmen, previously detailed, man the rigging and keep their eyes on the man in the water." Of course in a large vessel a boat is lowered at once.

To sum up: Always have a good life buoy at hand where it can be reached instantly, both when under way and when at anchor in a strong tideway. Drop it as close as possible to the man, between him and the boat, and then get back to him just as quickly as conditions will allow. Then get the way off the boat so that she will not drive on past him, or, worse yet, run him down. Have a clear idea of exactly what you are going to do, keep cool, and give any necessary orders in plenty of time and in clear, firm and unhurried tones. It is an exciting time, but the man's life may depend on your keeping your head and making your crew and passengers keep theirs.

THE ETIQUETTE OF YACHTING.

WHAT TO DO AND WHAT NOT TO DO WHEN ABOARD YOUR BOAT OR AT THE CLUB.

BY HERBERT L. STONE.

THE newcomer into the sport of yachting, which, of course, includes motor boating, is apt to be unfamiliar with the etiquette that prevails aboard ship, so that a short talk on what to do and what not to do should be valuable to him. There are many unwritten laws in the boating game, all of them based on sound reasoning and with the tradition of years back of them, and it is wise not to transgress these rules, either through neglect or ignorance of them.

In the first place, every man that does boating for pleasure should join some good yacht club. Not only does it give him a place where he can keep his boat and which he can use as his boating headquarters, but it gives him privileges at other yacht clubs when cruising which he would not otherwise have, and brings him into touch with other boat owners whose interests are in many ways identical with his own.

A club also offers the advantages of a boatman to look after your boat, usually for a small fee; has facilities for hauling out and cleaning off the bottom, for making any minor repairs, and frequently provides storage accommodations for the winter. The advantages that one gets from a yacht club will more than compensate for the cost of becoming a member.

While as a rule a yacht club has no exclusive privilege to the anchorage in front of its clubhouse, the use of such anchorage is usually conceded to the members of that club, and it is not good etiquette to plant a permanent mooring in a choice position in front of a clubhouse without being a member of the club.

While nearly all other yacht clubs extend the privilege of their clubhouse and float to members of other recognized yacht clubs while cruising, one should not abuse this privilege by using a club in this manner for a long period of time. It is all right for a visiting yachtsman to drop anchor off a clubhouse of which he is not a member and use its float, and its clubhouse if privileges are extended to his own club, for a week or possibly two weeks, but if one stays longer than that he is apt to outlast his welcome.

In coming to an anchorage in front of a strange club, be careful not to drop your hook over someone else's permanent moorings and be sure that you do not anchor near enough to any other boat so that there is danger of fouling when the boats swing with wind or tide. A stranger should also be careful about coming to a yacht club float with a power boat and lying there any length of time, blocking off the float from any one who may want to get in or out. Also, in landing at a club float with your dinghy do not leave the boat tied to the front of the float, but take it out around to the back and make it fast where it will be out of the way. Clubs often provide a separate float for the storing of dinghies, or a line of moorings to which they can be made fast, and a visitor should always inquire as to this before leaving the float.

A stranger should always be careful to avoid anchoring in a channel in a strange harbor. Some of our clubs are located on small harbors and the channel being narrow, a single yacht may block it so that others cannot get in or out.

In selecting a mooring at your own club do not plant it in a position that some one else may have preëmpted, or have claimed by right of long occupancy. First comers always have first choice of moorings, and one should always consult the boatman in charge of the anchorage before planting his mushroom for the season. The same applies to anchoring, and one should not anchor where there is danger of fouling other boats that have anchored before him.

When at a visiting club the burgee of the club to which the visiting yacht belongs should always be flown from sunrise to sunset, as will be told later in the paragraphs on flag etiquette. Gun salutes should be avoided as much as possible. A lot of yachtsmen like to fire their small deck cannon at every available opportunity. It is a pernicious practice and should be discontinued.

In visiting other boats in the harbor one should be careful not to do so at meal times. This can always be told on yachts that fly meal pennants by the appearance of such a pennant at spreaders, or yard if a power boat. If these are not carried, meal hours can generally be guessed at or noted by the fact that all hands are below.

Don't pay more attention to your uniform than you do to the equipment of your yacht. On small boats uniforms are more or less out of place unless the owner happens to be the flag officer of some yacht club, and it always seems like presumption to see the owner of a 25-foot catboat or power boat come ashore with as much gold braid on his cap and coat as an officer of the navy.

A FEW DON'TS.

Here are a few "don'ts" which the late dean of American yachting, Mr. A. Cary Smith, recently set down for the benefit of those who would be *persona grata* aboard of a yacht:

Don't wear resounding garments.

Don't sport prismatic hose.

Don't wear sleeveless shirts; they are an abomination in the eyes of all sailormen.

Don't bring on board a kit bag like a cow's belly with a handle to it.

Don't point at other boats and make remarks about the wind.

Don't say you would like a cocktail.

Don't pick out a place in the shade.

Don't be afraid to sit on the wet deck.

Don't sit near the wheel.

Don't touch gear that you know nothing about.

Don't speak if there is a mixup.

Don't speak to the captain.

Don't be too free with the booze when you go to lunch—if there is any.

Don't be afraid to tail on the main sheet or other gear that you understand.

Don't forget what Count Considine said to Charley O'Malley: "All men are equal before the pistol."   The same is true race day.

If these precepts are followed you will get the "glad hand" from the owner and the respect of the crew, not to mention many days of keen sport in the future.

The following is the usual rule of flag routine on board of yachts. If one flies flags at all he should be punctilious about them.

DISTINGUISHING FLAGS AND WHERE THEY SHOULD BE FLOWN.

(New York Yacht Club Regulations.)

The distinguishing marks of a yacht in commission, other than the yacht ensign, are a burgee and flag or private signal. On sailing yachts, when under way, the yacht ensign should be displayed at the main peak of single and of two-masted yachts, at the mizzen-peak of three-masted yachts and at the mizzen-gaff of ketches and yawls. Steam or other power yachts should fly the yacht ensign from a staff at the stern. When at anchor, the yacht ensign should be displayed from a staff at the stern of all yachts, other than ketches and yawls, where it should be displayed at the mizzen-truck. On a yacht with two or more masts, the burgee is flown at the fore-truck and the private signal at the main. When under way, single-masted yachts, other than ketches and yawls, should fly the owner's private signal at the main truck; when at anchor, the burgee. On ketches and yawls, the private signal should be flown at the mizzen and the burgee at the main.

On a mastless yacht, the distinguishing flag is flown at the loftiest or most conspicuous hoist, but the burgee and private signal should *never* be flown on the same hoist. The distinguishing flag of a Flag Officer is always flown at the main both day and night. The Club burgee and private signal may be "made up" and mast-headed previous to colors and "broken out" when the signal for colors is given, but the ensign should *never* be "made up" and "broken out."

YACHT ROUTINE.

(Adopted by the Leading Yacht Clubs of the United States.)

COLORS, ETC.—Yachts in commission should hoist their colors at 8 o'clock A. M., and haul them down at sunset, taking time from the senior officer present.

Before colors in the morning and after colors at sunset, the ensign and distinguishing flags should be shown when entering port, and should be hauled down immediately on coming to anchor.

At all other times yachts should fly a night pennant at the main, from colors at sunset until colors the next morning.

No guns should be fired for colors except by the yacht giving the time, nor from colors at sunset until colors the next morning, nor on Sunday.

Absence flags and meal pennants are not considered colors.

On Decoration Day and occasions of national mourning the ensign only should be half-masted. On the death of the owner of the yacht, both the club flag and his private signal should be half-masted, but not the ensign. When mourning is ordered for the death of a member of the club, the club flag only should be half-masted. This rule should apply to yachts both at anchor and under way.

Flags should always be mast-headed before half-masting them, and should be mast-headed before hauling them down. Saluting with the ensign at half-mast should be done by mast-heading first.

In making colors, salutes, etc., the yacht always represents the rank of the owner, whether he is aboard or not.

PENNANTS, PRIVATE SIGNALS, ETC.—Flag officers should always fly their pennants while in commission.

Yachts, when the owner is not on board,

should fly at the main starboard spreader, during daytime, a blue flag, rectangular in shape. This flag should never be flown when under way.

Single-masted vessels should fly the private signal of the owner when entering a home port, or when approaching other yachts at sea; at other times the club flag, except when with the squadron.

OFFICER IN COMMAND OF ANCHORAGE.—The senior officer present should be in command of the anchorage, should give the time for colors, make and return salutes, visits, etc.

His yacht should remain the station vessel until a senior to him in rank arrives and assumes the command of the anchorage.

MEAL PENNANTS.—A white flag, rectangular in shape, should be flown at the main starboard spreader on schooners, and at the starboard spreader on single-masted vessels, during the meal hours of the owner.

A red pennant pointed in shape should be flown at the fore-port spreader on schooners, and at the port spreader on single-masted vessels, during the meal hours of the crew. A white light should be displayed on starboard spreader after sunset and during owner's meal hours.

LIGHTS. — *Commodore.* — From colors at sunset until sunrise the commodore should show, when on board, two blue lights, perpendicularly, at the stern; when absent, one blue light should be shown.

Vice-Commodore. — The vice-commodore should show lights as provided for the commodore, substituting red lights instead of blue.

Captains. — Captains, when on board, should show a white light under the main boom; when absent this light should be extinguished.

SALUTES. — All salutes should be returned in kind.

The following rules should not apply to yachts leaving for, or returning from a day's sail:

Yachts should salute vessels of the United States Navy by dipping the ensign once.

The commodore, on entering port to join the squadron, should be saluted, on coming to anchor, by the yachts present. On all other occasions the commodore should be saluted, on coming to anchor, by the officer in command.

Junior flag officers should be saluted, on coming to anchor, by the officer in command, unless the latter be a senior in rank, in which case they should salute him.

Captains should on all occasions salute the officer in command.

The salute from yachts entering port should be made by dipping the ensign once, or by firing a gun on letting go anchor.

The senior officer, when leaving the anchorage, excepting temporarily, should indicate the transfer of command to the next in rank by firing a gun on getting under way. All other yachts should salute the officer in command.

All visits should be made according to rank.

Yachts, passing one another, should always exchange salutes by dipping the ensign once, junior saluting first. Steam whistles should never be used to make salutes.

The salute to yachts entering port, entitled to a salute, should be made by dipping the ensign once, or by firing a gun, when they let go anchor.

An official salute to a foreign club should be made by firing a gun, with the flag of the foreign club at the fore on schooners and steamers, and at the main on single-masted vessels; or, in the absence of such flag, by half-masting the club flag and firing a gun. When the salute has been returned, or a reasonable time for its return allowed, the flag should be hauled down, and the club flag hoisted again.

The salute from or to yachts arriving after sunset, or on Sunday, should be made immediately after colors on the following morning.

When a flag officer makes an official visit, a gun should be fired, with his pennant at the fore on schooners and steamers, and at the main on single-masted vessels, while he remains on board.

A yacht, acting as judges' boat, should not be saluted during a race.

The quarter-deck should always be saluted by lifting the cap on coming on board or from below.

WITH THE SQUADRON.—Yachts should report to the commanding officer on joining the squadron, and should obtain his permission before leaving it.

When under way with the squadron, firing guns and signaling should be avoided, except when joining or parting company, or when repeating signals.

Passing at Sea.—When squadrons of different clubs meet at sea, salutes should be exchanged only by the commanding officers.

Salutes from single yachts at sea should only be answered by the flag-ship.

Single-masted vessels should fly the private signal of the owner when under way with the squadron; when at anchor, the club flag.

When a foreign yacht arrives, the senior officer present should send on board, without regard to rank, a tender of the civilities of the club.

ENTERING A FOREIGN PORT.—Yachts should salute on entering port in the home waters of a foreign club, where any of its fleet are lying.

After the tender of civilities has been made, owners of the entering yachts should visit the officer in command of the anchorage. All other visits should be made according to rank—visits to their equals in rank being made by the owners of the entering yachts.

The time for colors in the home waters of a foreign club should be given with its senior flag officer present.

The term "foreign" should be understood as applying to all other clubs outside of the waters in which a club is stationed.

Made in the USA
Middletown, DE
15 June 2021